Unlocking the Secrets
-to- Scorpios

Unlocking the Secrets -to- Scorpios

*How People of Every Sign Can Effectively Handle
the Scorpios in Their Lives*

Trish MacGregor

renowned astrologer and award-winning author

PAGE STREET
PUBLISHING CO.

PAGE STREET
PUBLISHING CO.

Copyright © 2015 Trish MacGregor
First published in 2015 by
Page Street Publishing Co.
27 Congress Street, Suite 103
Salem, MA 01970
www.pagestreetpublishing.com

Distributed by Macmillan; sales in Canada by The Canadian
Manda Group.

18   17   16   15   1   2   3   4   5

ISBN-13: 978-1-62414-153-9
ISBN-10: 1-62414-153-6

Library of Congress Control Number: 2015938189

Cover and book design by Page Street Publishing Co.

Printed and bound in the United States

Page Street is proud to be a member of 1% for the Planet.
Members donate one percent of their sales to one or more of the
over 1,500 environmental and sustainability charities across the
globe who participate in this program.

This one is for Rob & Megan
with love always

Contents

How to Use This Book

You probably have a Scorpio in your life and may not even know it! According to www.statisticbrain.com, nearly 10 percent of the population is a Scorpio, making it the most common zodiac sign. Whether the Scorpio in your life is a friend or colleague, a spouse or lover, a boss, parent or a child, you'll find information and advice in this book about how to navigate this complex relationship effectively and peacefully.

Anyone born between October 23 and November 21 is a Scorpio. If the Scorpio you know was born on October 22 or 23, then that person is "on the cusp" and may exhibit Libra traits and behaviors. His or her personality could be a blend of the two signs. If the person was born at the tail end of the Scorpio cycle—November 21 or 22—then he or she is on the cusp between Scorpio and Sagittarius and will exhibit traits of both signs. But because Scorpio is such a powerhouse, there will be an abundance of traits and behaviors in this person that are readily identifiable as Scorpio.

No one, however, is just a sun sign. There may be someone in your life who you have pegged as a Scorpio, only to discover the person is a Pisces or a Leo, but has a moon, rising or a cluster of planets in Scorpio. Regardless, the Scorpio intensity will shine through!

This book will shed some light on the mystery of Scorpio and provide you with tips and guidance so that all of your interactions with Scorpios can be harmonious and beneficial for you both. So dive into the exciting world that is Scorpio, and enjoy the journey!

Introduction

Astrology & Synchronicity

At the moment you drew your first breath, the stars in the heavens were at particular positions in the sky. Perhaps the sun was in Scorpio, the moon in Gemini, Mercury in Libra, and on through the solar system lineup, right out to Pluto. The signs these planets occupied represented an archetypal energy—your potential—and created a pattern intrinsic to the instant you were born. These patterns are how synchronicity comes into play with astrology.

Swiss psychologist Carl Jung, who coined the term synchronicity, defined it as the "coming together of inner and outer events in a way that can't be explained by cause and effect and is meaningful to the observer." In other words, meaningful coincidence.

Jung first wrote about the concept in 1949, in the introduction to Richard Wilhelm's translation of *The I Ching* or *Book of Changes*, a divination system that is at least 5,000 years old. The *I Ching* is based on sixty-four patterns known as hexagrams that are derived by tossing three coins six times. The pattern created when the coins are tossed is, like the pattern created when you were born, inherent to the moment. A birth chart, like a hexagram, forms a meaningful blueprint of archetypal potential. The signs in which the planets fall, the angles or aspects they make to each other, the phase of the moon and the planets that were rising or setting all hold significance.

Mainstream scientists and educators dismiss astrology as a superstition of the past and see astronomy as the science of celestial bodies. But Galileo, the father of modern astronomy, was also an astrologer. He was attacked by the church for his astrological predictions and spent much of his life under house arrest. In spite of efforts through the centuries to discredit astrology, it's a vibrant means of analyzing personalities and relationships and predicting the future. Some scientists, in fact, have been startled by its accuracy.

In 1950, French statistician Michel Gauquelin embarked on a singular crusade to prove that the birth positions of stars and planets don't exert any influence on a person's future development. But his own statistics proved him wrong. He found that great soldiers, military leaders and warlords tended to have Mars rising in their horoscopes. The odds of this being pure chance were five million to one.

"In Jungian terms, the astrological evidence suggests that the collective unconscious is ultimately embedded in the macrocosm itself, with the planetary motions a synchronistic reflection of the unfolding archetypal dynamics of the human experience," wrote Richard Tarnas in *Cosmos and Psyche: Intimations of a New World View.*

Jung also coined two other words that are vital to understanding how astrology works: *archetype* and the *collective unconscious.* Archetypes represent our common experiences as human beings. The collective unconscious is like the DNA of the human race, a psychic repository of our history as a species. It contains archetypal images that are common to all people regardless of cultural background, nationality, ethnicity or religious beliefs. These images are found in mythology, folklore, fairy tales, legends, dreams, hallucinations and fantasies. Mother, father, child, family, wise old man or woman, animal, hero, trickster, shadow and persona are the most universal images.

So when we talk about the archetypal energy of a sun sign, we're referring to overall personality traits. All of us are more than our sun signs, of course, but because the sun is the very energy and essence of life, it's a particularly powerful and accurate indicator of who you are. In astrology, the sun symbolizes the Self, the ego—your individuality. Its energy is yang. To some extent, your sun sign symbolizes your creative ability, authority, personal power, general state of physical health and strengths and weaknesses of the physical body.

Interestingly, according to data released in 2014 from the National Science Foundation's *Science and Engineering Indicator* study, the percentage of Americans who think astrology isn't at all scientific declined from 62 percent in 2010 to 55 percent in 2012. The NSF reports that Americans are less skeptical of astrology than they have been at any time since 1983.

Why?

Perhaps part of it is that in tumultuous times, it's natural to seek insight and guidance about decisions we must make, paths we should follow and dreams we might pursue. It's empowering to understand how our particular sun signs are endowed with certain strengths we haven't mined, certain creative talents we may not have tapped yet. And, yes, sun signs shed light on issues of compatibility, romance, who we may fall in love with or marry, or why we do or don't get along with a sibling, boss, parent, child or business partner.

That said, your sun sign—and your natal chart—represent *potential*, not *fate*. We are masters of our own destinies who write the script of our lives from the inside out, based on our core beliefs, intentions and desires. Over the years I've been practicing astrology, I have come to believe that we actually choose it all. Before we're born, our souls, higher selves or whatever you want to call it, choose the circumstances into which we're born—our parents, the issues we should work on in each lifetime and the optimal astrological conditions that will allow us to develop and evolve spiritually, creatively and emotionally, on every level. These conditions are external expressions of internal needs and help create the reality we experience. But our free will reigns supreme.

As you work with this concept, you realize that everything that happens to you—from the grand to the mundane—is the result of a belief you hold. If it's your belief, you can change it. If you change the core belief, your experience also changes, and this is what empowers you as an individual.

A Little Test

The zodiac consists of twelve signs and each sign contains thirty degrees. The degree the sun occupied when you were born often corresponds to a year in your life when some sort of transformative experience occurred within the first thirty years of your life. It could be any defining event—a birth or death, a marriage or divorce, an accident or illness, a move, a first job or a new love. The timing isn't always exact—give it a leeway of about six months on either side.

My natal sun is sixteen degrees twelve minutes of Gemini. Five months after my sixteenth birthday, my parents moved from Venezuela, where I was born and raised, to the U.S. This event was huge for me, transformative, and defined much of the rest of my life. It also prompted me to look for answers in unconventional places—like astrology.

If you don't know the degree of your sun sign, you can find it—and get a free natal chart—at www.astro.com. The symbol for the sun is a circle with a dot in the center. This small test is one you can conduct on your own to prove the veracity of astrology.

A Few Astro Basics

The twelve signs are divided into two categories: triplicities or elements and quadruplicities or modes.

The elements—fire, earth, air and water—describe the fundamental energy and consciousness of a particular sign. It's the lens through which individuals of that sign perceive the world. The energies of these elements are manifested through the vibrational frequencies of the modalities: cardinal, mutable and fixed. They express the ways we use this energy. Each sign is classified by both its element and its modality.

The Elements

Fire: Aries, Leo, Sagittarius

The nature of fire is to burn. But fire exists in many forms: candlelight, fireworks, brush fires, solar flares, explosions, fire from a match, in a fireplace and forest fires. We use fire for light, for cooking our food and for warmth. It's all the same energy, but whether it's constructive or destructive depends on the way we use it.

As a group, fire signs are energetic, passionate, enthusiastic, dramatic, impulsive, impetuous and filled with vitality. They're the Indiana Jones of the zodiac. They're action-oriented—great at starting things and getting projects off the ground. They're innovators and paradigm-busters. They can also be emotionally explosive, sharp-tongued and consumed by their own energies.

Earth: Taurus, Virgo, Capricorn

The earth signs are calmer than their fire cousins. These folks are grounded, efficient and pay attention to details. Pragmatism is their middle name. It's unlikely that an earth sign would head off to Tahiti on the spur of the moment. But a Sagittarian would do it in a heartbeat, with nothing more than a backpack and his ATM card.

Earth signs enjoy gardening, sports, camping and being outdoors. They tend to be athletic and often enjoy cooking and gourmet foods. They can be security conscious, ambitious individuals, but always move at their own leisurely pace, which can drive everyone around them crazy.

Air: Gemini, Libra, Aquarius

In some ways, the air signs are the most ephemeral of the zodiac, the hardest to pin down. We can see fire, earth and water, but not air. However, we perceive the effects of air—a sea breeze, wind blowing through trees, hurricanes, tornadoes, La Niña, El Niño, smog and fog. Then there's the simple fact that if we don't breathe, we die.

The mind is the air sign's domain, and it's through the mind that these individuals explore their emotions. This may seem contradictory, since we usually don't think of emotions as a mental process. But for an air sign, it isn't enough to just feel something; they have to *understand* it, and that's the job of the mind. They excel at language, communication and abstract thought. They are networkers.

Water: Cancer, Scorpio, Pisces

We drink it, swim in it and bathe in it. It feeds our lawns, our flowers and our slice of earth. It covers most of our planet and 65–75 percent of our bodies, depending on our age, health, weight and gender. It molds itself to whatever vessel contains it. Like air, we can't live without it.

Water signs are about intuition and emotion. They *feel* their way through life; it's the lens through which they see the world. When they emote excessively, they become the smothering parent, the infidel, the martyr or the savior in our midst. Water signs can be so intense that they radiate energy that people around them can feel. Always, there's a sense that they're connected to something larger, that they know stuff that eludes the rest of us. And, quite often, they do. They are the natural psychics of the zodiac.

The Modalities

Cardinal: Aries, Cancer, Libra, Capricorn

Innovators, initiators and generally sociable. These individuals tend to move in one direction, along a single, focused path. They are initiators who use their energy in highly specific ways. They aren't quitters, unless they lose interest in something. Then they walk away without apology or regret.

Mutable: Gemini, Virgo, Sagittarius, Pisces

Adaptable, flexible, communicators and networkers. Mutable signs are the most adaptable in the zodiac and fit in nearly anywhere because they easily adjust to the moods and emotions of the people around them. They are masters of camouflage and can converse with anyone about anything.

Fixed: Taurus, Leo, Scorpio, Aquarius

Stubborn, persistent, set in opinions and industrious. These individuals are slow to change their convictions just because someone tells them something is true or false. *Prove it to me*, is one of their mantras. While the other person is trying to prove it, they set out on their own quest for truth.

Since this book is specifically about Scorpio, let's get started and explore this powerful, secretive and often inscrutable sign.

Chapter 1:

Scorpio: The Transformer

October 23-November 21

"Be careful what you pretend to be
because you are what you pretend to be."
- Kurt Vonnegut, November 11

Secretive. Powerful emotions. Passionate. Sexual. Piercing insights. Regeneration. Destruction. Rebirth. Resurrection. These words are often used to describe Scorpio, a fixed water sign, and while all of them are true, they aren't the full story.

Scorpio's intense and sweepingly powerful emotions often make him feel as if he's been seized by a force beyond his control. In spite of how he feels, this sense of outside forces is just an illusion. His emotions are his allies. They provide him with an immediate and direct connection to the deepest parts of his intuitive self and are capable of instantly transforming his reality.

This transformation occurs when he brings his considerable will, intent and burning desire to bear against whatever it is that he wants to change. When his energy is so laser-focused and backed with passion, this change occurs at the quantum level and can result in the remission of an illness or disease, sudden rise to wealth and fame, an explosion of psychic ability or landing the dream job. His reality changes—and can do so in a heartbeat.

His emotions permeate everything he does, every choice he makes, every thought he thinks and every dream he has. They are the lens through which he perceives himself and his world. And sometimes they nearly overwhelm him.

Scorpio is also about power—the power he wields over others and the power others wield over him. This power is sometimes misused and then its tremendous capacity for positive transformation turns negative. Self-awareness is what spells the difference. Take Charles Manson and Bill Gates. The only thing these two men have in common is that both are Scorpios. Manson wielded his power in such a profoundly evil way, and Gates wielded his power to transform the world in an overwhelmingly positive way.

Stats

According to www.statisticbrain.com, as of 2012, the most common zodiac sign is Scorpio. Scorpios make up 9.6 percent of the population. Virgo follows in at a close second at 9.4 percent of the population and then Gemini at 9.3 percent. What about the other nine signs?

Pisces – 9.1%	Aries – 8.1%
Libra – 8.8%	Sagittarius – 7.3%
Cancer – 8.5%	Leo – 7.1%
Taurus – 8.3%	Aquarius – 6.3%
Capricorn – 8.2%	

Because Scorpio doesn't accept easy answers about anything and always looks for her own truth, she tends to dig and probe deeply into whatever she takes on: a relationship, a creative project, a cure for some terrible disease or the answer to the riddle of the universe. She turns on that laser focus, frees her intuition, dives in and doesn't give up until she finds what she's looking for—the absolute bottom line.

Scorpio is probably one of the most misunderstood signs, often associated exclusively with intense sexuality. In fact, some descriptions of Scorpio that I've read over the years make her sound like a sex fiend or like some sort of primitive human who lurks through shadows and darkness in search of a sex partner. The truth is that sex just for the purpose of sex doesn't interest her as much as sex as a means to a deeper kind of knowledge about her partner. She's after the *whys* and *whats* that have molded her partner, and sex is a means of uncovering that. Even when she's involved in a relationship that is strictly sexual, there are always more dimensions to the relationship for her.

The other element that is so often associated with Scorpio is secrecy, but it's due to a lack of trust and a reluctance to let just anyone into the privacy of her head, the sanctuary of her being. People must win her trust, and it isn't easily won. Beneath her smoldering sexuality and piercing insights lies a toughness that others may sense but may not be able to define. She's an enigma even to the people who know her well, and much of the time she's a mystery to herself as well.

Instead of Asking, "What Sign Are You?"

If you feel that someone in your life is a Scorpio but you don't want to ask what his or her sign is, there are ways to tell:

➤ *His eyes.* Scorpio's eyes are often intense, with a piercing quality. He looks at you in a way that makes you feel he's peering into your soul.

➤ *Her interests.* Does she talk about the paranormal? Things that go bump in the night? The weird and the strange? Is she preoccupied with death or life after death? What kinds of books does she read? What kinds of movies does she like? *The Lovely Bones* or the Harry Potter books and movies would be more her taste than *Birdman*.

➤ *His voice.* Scorpios often have low, husky voices or seductive voices.

➤ *Her presence.* Every Scorpio generates a powerful sense of presence.

Planetary Rulers:

Pluto and Mars

Every sign is ruled by a planet, and some signs, like Scorpio, also have a co-ruler. These rulers are associated with mythological gods and goddesses whose lives and personalities match the tone and texture of a particular sign. Ancient astrologers assigned Mars as Scorpio's ruler. But with the discovery of Pluto in 1930, modern astrologers assigned that planet to rule Scorpio.

To the ancient Greeks, Mars was Ares, a savage god who was little more than a thirsty SOB. In the *Iliad*, Zeus says it as he sees it. He finds Ares, his son, completely odious because his primary enjoyments are nothing but "strife, war, and battle." On Olympus, Ares was disliked for his blind violence and brutality. He was all about aggression, physicality and survival.

The ancient Romans looked upon Mars much more kindly. They called him by the name we know him, and he was first and foremost the god of agriculture, the protector of cattle and the preserver of corn. As the husband of Rhea Silvia, a vestal virgin, he fathered Romulus and Remus, who were suckled by a wolf.

The connection between Mars and sex probably came about because of Ares's affair with the goddess Aphrodite. At the time, she was married to a cripple, Hephaestus, and compared to him, Ares was a dashing suitor, handsome and utterly fearless—all the things the Olympians looked for in a mate. Ares, naturally, took advantage of the situation. All the other gods eventually discovered their lustful encounters when Hephaestus ensnared the adulterous couple in an invisible net.

These ancient mythological gods had strange and dramatic lives, fraught with all the sexual and emotional tension of soap operas, and Mars/Ares certainly had his share. He was assigned as the ruler of Scorpio until the discovery of Pluto in 1930 by a young astronomer named Clyde Tombaugh.

Tombaugh and his fellow astronomers were certain he had discovered the long suspected ninth planet in the solar system, the mysterious Planet X. In classical mythology, Pluto governed the underworld, or Hades, as it was known when referring to an actual place. For the Greeks, Pluto was seen as more benefic than the ruler of hell; he was the god who reigned over the afterlife. Like all these mythological gods, his life was tumultuous, and he is probably best known as the dude who abducted Persephone and took her to the underworld—hardly a stunning endorsement of his character. That said, though, he apparently turned into a loving husband for Persephone.

Pluto's underworld and afterlife connections fit well with Scorpio's ability to delve into the unseen, the unknown and the mysterious, and also fits Scorpio's natural home, the eighth house, which governs death, the afterlife, reincarnation and the occult. So, eventually, Pluto became the modern ruler of this sign. Even though Pluto was demoted as a planet in 2006, astrologers who dismiss it do so at their own peril!

Scorpio's Creativity & Intuition

All signs have creative and intuitive strengths. We develop, nurture and use these talents, or we don't. But for Scorpio, there's no hesitation or ambivalence about what he'll do with his creative talents. He's all about breaking taboos, digging deeper, getting to the heart of whatever it is. And his considerable intuition is one of the vehicles through which he does this.

Imagine this. It's the late fifties, and life is as stark as a black-and-white photograph with good guys and bad guys clearly defined. Strict gender roles exist—men work and women don't—and hundreds of things are taboo and never enter polite conversation. Now imagine two young women, both aspiring poets. They meet at Boston University, where they're taking Robert Lowell's class in poetry. Lowell has already drawn analogies between the two students, perhaps noting that both women have a fascination with death. As the friendship between the women deepens, they share intimate details of their individual suicide attempts.

Their bond, this dangerous fascination with death, is incomprehensible to others. But after the younger of the two women kills herself, the other poet tells her shrink: "She took something that was mine, that death was mine. Of course it was hers, too. But we swore off it, the way you swear off smoking."

The women, Anne Sexton and Sylvia Plath, were both Scorpios, and this sign is about transformation at the deepest levels. For these two women, there wasn't any transformation as significant as creativity and death. Of the two, Sexton tackled taboos the way few other female writers had at the time. Her poems included taboos that ran the spectrum from abortion to menstruation, incest to adultery, masturbation to drug addiction.

During Anne Sexton's first psychiatric hospitalization, her psychiatrist urged her to resume writing poetry as a kind of therapy. She wrote some of her best pieces then, and some of them became her first published book, *To Bedlam and Part Way Back*. Most of her poetry reflected the probing intensity typical of Scorpio. Her fame grew out of her need to understand herself. By turning her emotions inside out, she won a Pulitzer Prize and was the first woman ever awarded an honorary Phi Beta Kappa from Harvard.

Famous Scorpios

As you'll see from this list, Scorpios aren't just famous to be famous. By following their passions, they transform the world.

Abigail Adams

John Adams

Hillary Clinton

Pat Conroy

Tim Cook

Michael Crichton

Marie Curie

Leonardo DiCaprio

Jodie Foster

Bill Gates

Edwin Hubble

Margaret Mitchell

Pablo Picasso

Sylvia Plath

Theodore Roosevelt

Carl Sagan

Jonas Salk

Anne Sexton

Kurt Vonnegut

A Scorpio's Intuition

Author Kurt Vonnegut regaled readers with his unusual novels—*Cat's Cradle*, *Breakfast of Champions*, *Slaughterhouse-Five* and others—that were a blend of satire, dark humor and science fiction. He was a Scorpio, born November 11, 1922, so it isn't surprising that when his intuition kicked in, he acted on it.

One morning in the days before the Internet and cell phones, he felt a sudden impulse to call his brother-in-law, whom he'd never phoned before and had no reason to call. "I suddenly left my study ... walked the length of my house to the phone in the kitchen, put in a long distance call to my brother-in-law," he told author Alan Vaughan in his book *Patterns of Prophecy*.

As the phone rang at the other end, Vonnegut heard a breaking news report on the radio about a train that had plunged off an open drawbridge in New Jersey. Even though his brother-in-law never rode the train, Vonnegut immediately knew he was one of the passengers on that doomed train. Within an hour, Vonnegut was headed to New Jersey, where his sister was hospitalized with terminal cancer and her four children were now fatherless.

Before the sun set that day, Vonnegut had taken charge of his sister's household and her kids. She died the next day. "My wife and I have since adopted and raised their children."

Scorpio's intuition may kick in, as Vonnegut's did, with an *impulse* to do something he has never done before. Rather than dismissing the impulse, Scorpio acts on it.

Once Scorpio has found her creative path, she often *becomes* the path, so that her life and her creative work are inseparable.

Or take Michael Crichton, another Scorpio. In an interview years ago, Crichton talked about the way he works. First, he researches. Scorpios excel at research. Over the course of Crichton's writing career, he delved into neurobiology, biophysics, primatology, UFOs, international economics, Nordic history, time travel and genetics. Once his research was completed, he started writing. He would get up early to write, take a lunch break and then return to his writing. As the book progressed, he would get up earlier and earlier until he wasn't sleeping at all. This kept the momentum rolling, and he would finish the book in about a month.

This kind of intense creativity is a hallmark of Scorpio, and is nearly as consistent in his life as his intuitive perceptions. The final chapter in the book goes into Scorpio's creativity in greater depth.

A Scorpio Natal Chart

The Houses

Before you take a look at Kurt Vonnegut's natal chart, you should understand a few basics about a birth chart and familiarize yourself with the glyphs or symbols for each of the planets. You'll find reference to "Nodes," which aren't planets but are the degrees where the plane of the moon's orbit crosses the ecliptic—the earth's orbit around the sun. The Nodes are about our connections with other people. The North Node, by sign and house placement, is the direction in which you should move in this lifetime to achieve all the potential promised in your chart. The South Node is what you have achieved in previous lives, your comfort zone.

A chart is divided into 12 houses, and in Vonnegut's chart, you'll see the number for each house on the inner ring of the circle. The horizontal line just above the first and seventh houses forms the horizon and is known as the ascendant or rising. The vertical line between houses nine and ten and three and four is the meridian. Entire books have been written about the houses in astrology, but the basics are fairly simple:

Ascendant or rising: Your entry point into this lifetime. It represents how other people perceive you, the mask you wear and the persona you project.

1st house: YOU, your physical appearance, general health, how you deal with the world, early childhood, ego and your creative thrust

2nd house: Your money and financial resources, how you earn your money, your material security and attachments and personal values

3rd house: Communication skills, siblings, short trips, your neighborhood, conscious mind in daily life, exchange of information and your intellect

4th house: Your home and domestic environment, early childhood conditioning, the nurturing parent, your roots, conditions at the end of your life and real estate

5th house: Children (particularly the first born), creative pursuits, pleasure, romance, love affairs and pets

6th house: Working conditions and environment, employees, competence and skill and maintenance of your daily health

7th house: Partnerships (both romantic and business), your spouse, open enemies and contracts

8th house: Joint finances and resources, taxes, death, inheritances, sexuality as transformation, your secrets, your partner's finances, metaphysics and the occult and psychic ability

9th house: The higher mind, higher education, law, philosophy and religion, foreign cultures, countries and travel, publishing and spiritual pursuits and interests

10th house: Profession and career, your public persona, authority figures, the authoritarian parent, status and position in the world and creative goals and achievements

11th house: Friends and associates, peer groups, social circles, your network of acquaintances and dreams and aspirations

12th house: Personal unconscious, hidden enemies, institutions (like hospitals, prisons, nursing homes), confinement, issues brought in from other lives and the power you have disowned and that must be claimed again

The Planets & the Nodes

☉	Sun	♃	Jupiter
☽	Moon	♄	Saturn
☿	Mercury	♅	Uranus
♀	Venus	♆	Neptune
♂	Mars	♇	Pluto
☊	North Node	☋	South Node

The Signs

♈	Aries	♎	Libra
♉	Taurus	♏	Scorpio
♊	Gemini	♐	Sagittarius
♋	Cancer	♑	Capricorn
♌	Leo	♒	Aquarius
♍	Virgo	♓	Pisces

Observations about Vonnegut's Chart

A complete analysis of Vonnegut's chart is beyond the scope of this book. However, notice the placement of his sun in the twelfth house, at 18 degrees Scorpio. When I first saw this, I wondered what defining event had occurred to Vonnegut when he was 18 years old and how this twelfth house sun had played out in his life. From biography.com, I learned that in 1940, at the age of 18, Vonnegut left home to attend Cornell. That event coincides with the degree of his sun. He was at Cornell until he enlisted in the army in 1942, and a year later he was sent to what is now Carnegie Mellon University to study engineering. The following year he was sent to Europe and fought in the Battle of the Bulge.

According to biography.com, "After this battle, Vonnegut was captured and became a prisoner of war. He was in Dresden, Germany, during the Allied firebombing of the city and saw the complete devastation caused by it. Vonnegut himself escaped harm only because he, along with other POWs, was working in an underground meat locker making vitamin supplements."

His confinement in prison fits with that twelfth house sun. It doesn't mean that everyone with the sun in the twelfth house will end up in prison, but that was how the energy manifested for Vonnegut. His experiences during the war provided creative fodder for his novels, another facet of this twelfth house sun. In *Slaughterhouse-Five*, the protagonist, Billy Pilgrim, is a soldier who, like Vonnegut, was taken prisoner and worked in a meat locker. True to the imaginative powers of a Scorpio sun in the twelfth house, Vonnegut's character begins to experience his life out of sequence and revisits different times repeatedly. He also encounters the Tralfamadorians, an alien race that exists in all times simultaneously. They kidnap Pilgrim and put him in a zoo on Trafalmadore with a Hollywood starlet, Montana Wildhack.

As biography.com noted, "This exploration of the human condition mixed with the fantastical struck a chord with readers, giving Vonnegut his first best-selling novel."

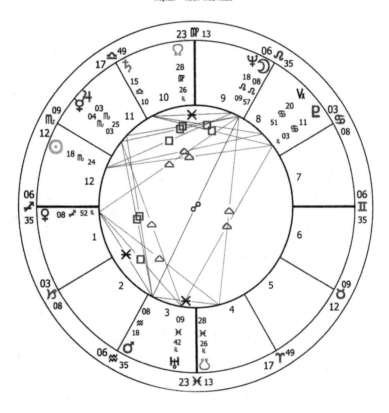

Kurt Vonnegut
Natal Chart
Saturday, November 11, 1922
8:00:00 AM CST
Indianapolis, Indiana
Tropical   Koch   True Node

Chapter 2:

Hooking Up with a Scorpio

"If you wish to make an apple pie from scratch,
you must first invent the universe."
—Carl Sagan, November 9

Dating a Scorpio is an experience you won't ever forget, regardless of how the relationship turns out. It's likely to be emotionally intense and passionate, sometimes secretive and rarely predictable. You may feel as if you're living in a John le Carré novel, propelled and buffeted by forces you don't fully understand. The source of Scorpio's raw power in romance acts as a kind of magnetism, and no sign is immune.

One of the first things you realize is that the relationship unfolds on Scorpio's terms, not yours. These individuals are strong-willed, resolute and accustomed to getting their own way. Gray areas don't exist for them. They live in black-and-white worlds, where everything is either/or, yes or no. In a relationship, it means that if you're ambiguous about what you feel, Scorpio will walk fast in the opposite direction. This sign doesn't have time for indecision.

Whether you're a guy dating a Scorpio woman or vice versa, it's smart to have your natal charts drawn up by a professional astrologer. By comparing the charts, an astrologer can pinpoint important connections, possible points of contention, why you're attracted to each other and how things between you may evolve.

The Swiss psychologist Carl Jung studied hundreds of charts of married couples back in the days before computers and astrological software, when charts were drawn up by hand, through complicated mathematical formulas. He concluded that the best relationships were those where the man and woman had the sun and moon, the sun and ascendant, or the sun and Venus or Mars conjunct—i.e., in the same signs.

If you have the pleasure of dating a Scorpio woman, you'll quickly notice that she smolders with a sexuality that turns heads on the street. The power of her presence seizes attention wherever she goes, wherever she is. If that stokes the beast of your jealousy, if you get possessive, then the relationship may be over before it even takes off. She can be jealous and possessive, however, and yes, that's something of a double standard. But don't even try to figure it out. Her motives, the passions that move her, are often inscrutable to others. She prefers it that way. Even if you asked her to explain herself—and she was willing to do so—she probably couldn't. So much of her exists in a place beyond language, in some deep intuitive current that guides and directs her life.

To capture her heart, be honest and up front from the beginning. And remember that if she ever catches you in a lie, she'll cut you off cold.

If you are dating a Scorpio man, you had better get ready for a roller-coaster ride. It will be the largest and most exciting roller coaster you've ever been on, with some of the steepest climbs and plunges you've ever known. But on the plateaus, on those gentle curves in the tracks, you will think you've died and gone to heaven.

The Scorpio man radiates presence as surely as his female counterpart. It can come across as a powerful sexuality that makes you melt inside with just a single glance. Or it can be something less definable, some compelling quality you can't quite articulate but that you feel in your blood and your bones.

In a dating relationship, he can sometimes come across as a control freak. But what's really going on, particularly in Scorpio men who are deeply intuitive or spiritually evolved, is that he's digging for answers about you. Are you worth his time and effort? How are the two of you the same? How are you different?

Give him time and space to figure it out. Play his game, but play it honestly, with all your cards on the table.

Aries Dating a Scorpio

Challenging but Passionate

As any fifth grade science student knows, fire and water don't mix. One extinguishes the other. But if we look at the internal chemistry of these two signs, this combination can usher in a relationship fueled by passion, adventure and unparalleled excitement. But Aries, there are some caveats to all this.

You, as a cardinal fire sign, tend to be all over the place in terms of your interests, creative pursuits and passions. As a fearless pioneer who lives like the *Star Trek* motto, you're terrific at initiating things. But you're not great at following things through and finishing them. You're outgoing and social and can work a room full of strangers with the ease of a politician. Scorpio, as a fixed water sign, tends to be more focused, finishes what he or she starts and delves much more deeply than you do. Let's take a closer look at how you can make this relationship work.

What You Need to Know

Your heart and soul are forever perched at the tip of your tongue. You open your mouth and out they tumble. It's how you are. But Scorpio is your opposite in this sense; so don't ever expect this sign to reciprocate.

Scorpio will listen. This sign is a great listener who mulls over all the information you have provided, all your stories and triumphs and defeats. But Scorpio won't confide in you until he or she is ready. Don't push or rush Scorpio. Don't get irritable. Go with the flow, Aries. Follow Scorpio's lead. Focus on the passions you share, whatever they are. One of those shared passions may be physical activity.

Rock climbing? Check.
Hiking? Check.
Whitewater rafting? Check.
Climbing Kilimanjaro? Check.
Sex? Double check.

You get the idea. Find the places where your interests intersect. Then follow the Dale Carnegie big three: don't criticize, condemn or complain.

When you're feeling restless and out of sorts, you rush around like it's your last day on the planet and you simply must accomplish everything you set out to do when you woke at 7:00 a.m. But it's not your last day, and everyone around you ends up feeling rushed and exhausted in your presence. If you do this with Scorpio, he or she will be long gone before the day ends.

In the Bedroom

You're both passionate people, and it's probably safe to say that you won't last more than a few dates before you hit the bedroom. And this is when everything is taken to a whole new level.

If you're the kind of Aries for whom sex is a rush toward completion, then you're in for a delightful surprise. For Scorpio, sex is a banquet of discovery, and the slower the better. So stretch it out, Aries. Set a mood for seduction. Whether it's a great home-cooked meal, a delicious wine, silk sheets—or all of the above—make it clear from the onset that you're ready to go wherever Scorpio leads you.

Relax into it. Understand that for Scorpio, sex isn't just about sex. It's about *connection* at a profound level, the level where you both may recognize that you have been together in past lives. At this cellular level, your souls speak to each other. Sex becomes a vehicle to a spiritual experience and bonding.

Scorpios, like every sign, are varied, and if the one you're dating indulges in sex and is gone without good-byes—or even coffee!—in the morning, then it's probably best for both of you to cut your losses and just walk away without regrets. If you're lucky, though, your date mate will be the banquet variety, slow and erotic.

What to Avoid

If you're dating a Scorpio, then this bullet list of don'ts may be the most important list you'll ever see.

- ➢ Don't whine.
- ➢ Don't complain.
- ➢ Don't be possessive.
- ➢ Don't demand answers.
- ➢ Don't accuse without facts.
- ➢ Don't lie.
- ➢ Don't pretend to be something you aren't.
- ➢ Don't act like you've got all the answers.
- ➢ Don't ignore Scorpio's contributions.
- ➢ Don't rush Scorpio.
- ➢ Don't ask impossible questions.

What to Embrace

Here's your second most important list. Always embrace:

- ➢ Sex
- ➢ Investigating the weird and the strange
- ➢ Scorpio's hunches (they're usually right on target)
- ➢ Emotional intensity—even when it makes you uncomfortable
- ➢ The beauty of silence (until you just can't stand it!)
- ➢ Creative approaches to everything

Compatibility

With Aries and Scorpio, the interests you share may not be readily apparent. You may want to take off on the spur of the moment with nothing more than your ATM card and a backpack. But Scorpio likes a bit more planning, thank you. Like a map, a GPS, an actual destination and how about some cash just in case the ATMs don't work? Your attitude may be that the fun lies in the journey. Scorpio probably agrees on that point, but for him the journey is a quest, movement toward understanding something in a deeper way. Your approaches differ, but your passions are similar.

The trick is to capitalize on your strengths as a couple and not fret about the details.

Making Scorpio Happy

Granted, you're not responsible for anyone's happiness or unhappiness. But if you choose to be in a relationship with a Scorpio, then keep in mind that most of them don't take well to reckless criticism. If you have something constructive to say, that's one thing. Scorpio will listen closely and take it to heart. But if you dislike the shoes Scorpio is wearing or the way she combs her hair or the outfit she's wearing, keep it to yourself. Besides, it's really none of your business.

Scorpio, like most signs, is happy when she's appreciated. Just be sure your appreciation is genuine. Her B.S. detector is exceptionally accurate.

Advice for Scorpio

Yes, the relationship with Aries can be challenging, Scorpio. His impatience, his spur of the moment travels and how easily he gets bored are enough to drive you nuts. But the lightning speed of his mind, his fearlessness, his athletic prowess and his passion for life certainly compensate!

Taurus Dating a Scorpio

Ideal

Earth and water. The chemistry sounds perfect, doesn't it? Water nourishes earth and earth holds and contains water. However, every sign has a polar opposite—Aries/Libra, Taurus/Scorpio, Gemini/Sagittarius and so on around the zodiac. This means that you and Scorpio occupy the same axis, are compatible in terms of elements, and share the same fixed sign modality. You are opposites, mirror images of each other.

You're a cultivator, Taurus, and Scorpio is an investigator. You perceive the world through a lens of practicality; Scorpio perceives everything through emotions and intuition. When this combination works, it does so because you and Scorpio balance each other. One possesses traits that the other doesn't.

While Scorpio is investigating, researching and probing into life's mysteries, you should be doing what you do best—cultivating your resources, pursuing your dreams and enjoying the beauty that surrounds you. It's risky to make Scorpio the center of your world. You can't *cultivate* this sign, but you can enrich and expand Scorpio's life in ways that benefit both of you.

What You Need to Know

You're a physical person who enjoys athletics, sports and pushing your body to its limits. You excel at working with your hands—gardening, woodworking, sculpting—and your eye for beauty is unequaled in the zodiac. Music often transports you into ethereal realms. Scorpio admires all of this about you.

But don't expect him to take yoga just because you love all those pretzel poses. Don't expect him to join your kickball team. His preference may be for more solitary activities—jogging, long walks in nature and pursuits that free his mind so that his emotions and intuition flow freely.

You often keep your emotions private. But if Scorpio asks you what's wrong, don't shrug it off. Verbalize what you feel. Once you start doing this, Scorpio is likely to reciprocate. This way, you won't experience any of those "bull rushes" when everything you've wanted to say and the accretion of petty annoyances suddenly explode out of you. Nothing turns a Scorpio off more quickly than a temper tantrum that seems to come out of the blue.

You're rarely in a hurry and that quality fits Scorpio's approach to life. Your patience, persistence and determination will work in your favor in this relationship. Both of you are looking for your soul mate, and when you find that other half, your commitment is probably for keeps.

The major challenge in this combination is that you are both incredibly stubborn. You'll either have to agree to disagree or find a way around it. Neither of you is very good at compromise.

In the Bedroom

Taurus is one of the most sensual signs in the zodiac and Scorpio one of the most sexual. The distinction between sensuality and sexuality may seem to be small, but it isn't. You, Taurus, find sensuality in anything that speaks to your senses—walking barefoot along a warm beach, eating exotic foods, listening to particular music, taking in an art exhibit and, of course, sex.

For you, sex is a sensual feast. For Scorpio, it's a venue for deeper communication, for delving into who you really are. In the bedroom, you two are evenly matched. Your biggest challenge in this area will be to stay out of the bedroom long enough to live the other parts of your lives!

Scorpio may not always be as romantic as you would like, Taurus, but this is easy to remedy. Instead of waiting for Scorpio to figure out how you enjoy being wined and dined, spell it out. Suggest dinner on a moonlit beach or a weekend getaway to a paradise you'll both enjoy. Be creative. Get wild. Scorpio will love it.

What to Avoid

If you list your own pet peeves, Taurus, chances are it's a close match to this bulleted list of what to avoid when you're dating a Scorpio.

- ➢ Don't argue over petty stuff.
- ➢ Don't make demands about commitment.
- ➢ Don't back Scorpio into a corner.
- ➢ Don't become dependent.
- ➢ Don't confront Scorpio about stuff that's none of your business.
- ➢ Don't violate personal privacy.
- ➢ Don't go through Scorpio's computer files, looking for passwords to Facebook and other social media sites.
- ➢ Don't jump to conclusions.
- ➢ Don't break up with Scorpio on Facebook!

What to Embrace

Well, this one is easy. Embrace:

- ➢ SEX
- ➢ The mystical, inexplicable and unknown
- ➢ Scorpio's intuition
- ➢ The bottom line

Compatibility

Nine-tenths of who you are, Taurus, lies beneath the surface. The same is true for Scorpio. Both of you have an innate sense of privacy. Both of you can be secretive. Secrecy isn't detrimental to a dating relationship unless you're hiding something from each other that would impact the relationship in a negative way. If, for instance, you have agreed to a sexually exclusive relationship and one of you has been unfaithful, then it's best to talk about it openly. Otherwise, what's the point in continuing to date?

You and Scorpio may find that you are stubborn about the same things. Politics, for instance. Maybe Scorpio is to the left of center and you're to the right. Or perhaps Scorpio follows an established religion or attends a particular church, and you don't believe in established religion. Neither of you will ever change each other's mind about either politics or religion, so if you can, agree not to discuss those areas. Focus on your strengths as a couple, on what works rather than on what doesn't work.

That's probably excellent counsel for all of us!

Making Scorpio Happy

No one is asking you to bend over backward to accommodate another person's needs and desires. But if you have feelings for Scorpio and think the dating relationship may develop into something else, then there are certain things you can do that will leave Scorpio smiling.

Join him in his favorite physical exercise, whatever it is. Dig into an area that intrigues him or that he's researching. When he does something beautiful for you—like bring you flowers or a gift—be appreciative. All too often, "thank you" is perfunctory for most of us, so when you say it to Scorpio, mean it. The same goes for those three words that you both long for: I love you.

Advice for Scorpio

Relax and enjoy all the beauty and goodwill that Taurus brings into your life. It really doesn't get much better than this, does it, Scorpio?

♊ + ♏
Gemini Dating a Scorpio

Never boring

As a mutable air sign ruled by Mercury, you're the communicator of the zodiac. Your approach to life is primarily intellectual and lies in the realm of ideas; Scorpio's approach is intuitive and lies in the realm of feelings and emotions. Air and water—a mutable sign and a fixed sign. Is there any hope for these two? Actually, there is, and with a few caveats, this combination can work quite well.

You're intrigued by Scorpio's ability to investigate and dig for answers, and Scorpio admires your ability to pull ideas out of thin air. There could be some great teamwork here for a business or creative venture, if both of you are so inclined. You're so versatile, Gemini, that keeping things interesting and varied in a dating relationship won't be a challenge, and Scorpio will enjoy the diversity. You tend to be more social than Scorpio, able to talk to anyone about virtually anything. But a steady diet of socializing will become tiresome for Scorpio, so strive for balance in this regard.

As a mutable sign, you're able to adapt quickly and easily, particularly in a fluid situation. Scorpio, as a fixed sign, is more likely to dig in his heels and refuse to change his mind or budge an inch. This tendency shouldn't be a problem unless you're the one who *always* gives in.

What You Need to Know

There's a good reason that Gemini's symbol is that of twins: you're as changeable as the weather and have two distinct sides to your personality. There's the Gemini who is upbeat, happy, social and curious about everything and everyone. Then there's the other twin whose mood plummets for no apparent reason at all. Scorpio may find this aspect of your personality bewildering—or tedious.

Depending on how serious the relationship is, you might explain why you're feeling down. Or, a simpler solution, just avoid Scorpio altogether when you're in one of these moods, particularly if she's the cause of your mood. If that's the case, discuss your grievance when you're feeling good again, and do it with your left-brain, analytical self in charge. If you come at Scorpio with an emotionally directed attack, the relationship will be over before the sun rises or sets.

In the Bedroom

Seduce my mind and I'm all yours. When it comes to sex, this is Gemini's litany. Any Scorpio worthy of the sign has the art of seduction pegged and can probably tell within five or ten minutes of a first date where you fall on the seduction scale, Gemini. Whatever your intellectual interests and passions—the esoteric, the paranormal, ancient sites, books, movies or cultural trends—Scorpio will identify it, hone in on it, and that will be that.

There are two distinct Gemini lovers. One won't linger in bed and the other one will. For the first twin, sex is a means of communication. It's a signal that the relationship has reached a more intimate level, that certain emotions are now engaged and that there is now a third entity in the relationship—US. For the second twin, sex is also a means of communication, but on a much deeper level. For this twin, the pillow talk where stories and secrets are exchanged is as important as the actual sex. For this twin, sex is a banquet in the same way that it often is for Scorpio. That's the twin who should be in the bedroom with Scorpio.

What to Avoid

We've all got pet peeves. But this list of things to avoid will bring a great equilibrium to your relationship with Scorpio.

> ➤ Don't talk just to fill the silence. Scorpio doesn't need the constant hum of conversation to feel bonded with you or close to you. A physical gesture can communicate that—holding hands, a quick hug or a kiss.
> ➤ Don't blame Scorpio for how you feel. All too often, many of us don't accept responsibility for our own feelings. We seek to lay the blame on others.
> ➤ Don't be something you aren't. Scorpio will see through that façade in a flash.
> ➤ Don't bend over backward to accommodate Scorpio. He'll think you're a pushover.
> ➤ Don't go back on your word. If you say you'll be somewhere at a certain time and cancel just because you feel like it, Scorpio won't be calling again.
> ➤ Don't commit unless your feelings are genuine.

What to Embrace

Pick up and peel an onion. Study each layer. What's at the core? It may be a cliché, but it's also true that Scorpio is as layered as an onion. As your dating relationship evolves, your natural curiosity, Gemini, will enable you to peel back those layers and learn who this person is at the core. Then again, depending on the Scorpio, you may peel and peel and never know the full truth. Often, Scorpio is an enigma even to herself. So in this process of getting to know Scorpio, embrace:

> ➤ The journey
> ➤ The discovery
> ➤ Scorpio's hunches and psychic insights
> ➤ Scorpio's relentless persistence to pursue knowledge in his own way
> ➤ What you learn about yourself in this journey

Compatibility

You and Scorpio are both in pursuit of knowledge; you simply have different methods of going about it. If you capitalize on each other's methods, a great balance will be struck, and what began as a dating relationship may expand into a business relationship as well. If you don't want to mix business and pleasure, that's fine. Take what you learn from Scorpio and put it to use in your own life.

Your compatibility for a prolonged relationship will depend on how you deal with a major difference between you. Your curiosity, Gemini, leads you all over the map. One day you're studying sculpture and the next week you're writing a novel, and two months from now, you're building websites. There's that constant restlessness, a continual networking, to try as many different things, to meet as many different people, as you can fit into one lifetime. Scorpio is far more focused on a particular area or interest and often finds that passion early in life. If the two of you can somehow make this difference work for you, then there's enough energy to keep this relationship going for a very long time.

Making Scorpio Happy

No one else can make Scorpio happy; he must do that on his own. But you can bring happiness into Scorpio's life in several significant ways. Be happy and content with yourself, with where you are in your life right now. Your point of power lies in the present. The present is your launch pad for creating the next moment and the next on up the line to decades in the future. You can't change the past, but you can forgive yourself for any transgressions you have committed in the past.

Advice for Scorpio

Let loose! Talk and communicate! And periodically, when you crave your solitude, just tell Gemini you need some down time, some alone time. She won't be offended, as long as you're honest.

Cancer Dating a Scorpio

Just about Perfect

A cardinal water sign and a fixed water sign. Two little peas in a pod. Does it get any better than this? Maybe not. Like Scorpio, you feel and intuit your way through the world. But there are some significant differences in your respective approaches.

You need roots, a safe harbor, a place to call your own. It may be a house in the suburbs, a shack on a beach or even a camper you live in. The camper would be the real life equivalent of the shell of the crab, the symbol for your sign; it's the house you carry with you. And, like the crab, you act and react emotionally by skittering sideways, which also allows you to avoid confrontation. Scorpio probably intuits all this about you, but won't necessarily understand it, at least not in a left-brain sort of way.

What You Need to Know

You generally don't feel comfortable discussing what you feel. Your sensitivity is often so heightened that you hide behind your protective, nurturing urges, tending to other people's needs rather than your own. You can be possessive, and in a dating relationship with a Scorpio this can be problematic.

Scorpio's intensity may overwhelm you at times. All that smoldering sexuality, that either/or mentality, can bewilder even less sensitive signs. On the other hand, your emotions can be just as intense at times. And, let's face it, isn't it a refreshing change to date someone whose mere presence urges you to take emotional risks you've avoided most of your life?

As a cardinal sign, you're terrific at initiating stuff, everything from ideas to projects to which concert you want to attend. But for you, like your Aries sibling, follow-through is a challenge. If you hit an obstacle, you may back off. Scorpio, though, usually finishes what he starts and when he runs into an obstacle, he finds a way around it—or busts through it. He, like other fixed signs, is in for the long haul. This area could be potentially difficult in a dating relationship.

In the Bedroom

If your attraction to Scorpio is visceral, and it may well be, then it won't be long before you're both eyeing the bedroom. And this is when you'll really get a sense of each other.

For you, sex is about connecting at a level beyond language. It's like stepping into the rushing river of your emotions and imagination and being swept into a kind of bliss. Sex can be the same thing for Scorpio, but don't forget that she's also learning who you are from the inside out. So invite her into the privacy of your shell, Cancer, and know that she'll never betray a confidence or a secret. What Scorpio learns about you stays with her. Sexually, just about anything goes for Scorpio—as long as it's genuine.

The area where you need to exercise caution, though, is mistaking sex as commitment or thinking you and Scorpio are now exclusive. It's best to discuss your respective expectations and boundaries, to verbalize things up front. Yes, this may be difficult for you, Cancer, but Scorpio will appreciate knowing where you're coming from.

What to Avoid

Most of us possess traits and behaviors that are irritating to other people. It's human nature. But if you want the relationship with Scorpio to go somewhere, here's a list of behaviors to avoid.

> ➢ Don't assume anything. If you're uncertain about something, ask. Scorpio will appreciate your honesty.
> ➢ Don't take Scorpio for granted.
> ➢ Don't break your word. If you tell Scorpio you'll be somewhere at a particular time, then be there, or call ahead of time to let her know why you can't make it.
> ➢ Don't lie for any reason. Even "little white lies" count as lies in Scorpio's book.
> ➢ Don't dump your entire past on Scorpio. Yes, your memories of the past are always vivid and real. You can recall what your Aunt Mary was wearing at that family barbecue twenty years ago and all the gritty details that led to it being a disaster. But Scorpio won't enjoy hearing about it.
> ➢ Don't inflict your dark moods on Scorpio. Park them in your closet.

What to Embrace

This list is the one to post on your fridge, a friendly reminder about what attracted you to Scorpio in the first place!

> ➢ Great conversation. Scorpio isn't a superficial conversationalist. When he talks, he's actually saying something and it's often deep, insightful and perhaps even profound.
> ➢ Terrific sex
> ➢ Emotional depth
> ➢ Steadfast persistence about nearly everything

And now feel free to add to this list, Cancer!

Compatibility

On a compatibility scale of one to ten, the Cancer/Scorpio combination is probably an eight. If one of you has a moon, Venus or Mars or an ascendant in the other's sun sign, then we're talking near perfect compatibility. That said, there is plenty in this combination upon which to build a solid, lasting relationship.

Your gentleness, Cancer, appeals to the softer side of Scorpio, that inner part of his being that seeks union and harmony with a partner. Scorpio's decisiveness speaks to that taciturn part of you that feels you'll never be understood or accepted as you are. In a dating relationship, you may discover that you have similar spiritual beliefs and creative talents that mix well. Capitalize on the commonalities that feel effortless.

Making Scorpio Happy

Let's be clear: it's not your job to make Scorpio happy, even if Scorpio sometimes thinks so. However, Scorpio is happiest when he's in the process of discovery, on a quest of some kind that enables him to connect a myriad of dots that elude less observant people. In this sense, your intuitive awareness and insights can be a tremendous help and will cement the bond between you.

If you're the type of Cancer who enjoys cooking—and many of them do and are excellent cooks—then know that a home-cooked meal goes a long way toward bolstering Scorpio's happiness.

Advice for Scorpio

Your energy can be overwhelming to a Cancer. So, always, Scorpio, treat him with the utmost gentleness and love.

Leo Dating a Scorpio

Wow, but...

Fire and water. Two fixed signs. Do they have a chance at a successful dating relationship? Absolutely, but with a few caveats.

Leo, you love being the center of attention, and will always play to an audience, even an audience of one. You have an innate sense of the dramatic and life is definitely your stage. That suits Scorpio just fine. He doesn't have any interest in playing to anyone and only asks that you keep the drama in your relationship to an absolute minimum.

As one of the romantics of the zodiac, you love being courted, wined and dined and being made to feel that you are the focus of your partner's attention. Scorpio will gladly accommodate you on all those levels. But be forewarned, Leo. This relationship isn't just about you. For things to work, you must give what you receive.

The challenging areas in this relationship may revolve around communication. You're up front about what you feel at any given moment, but Scorpio is far more circumspect. Also, as fixed signs, you're both fairly rigid in your opinions and beliefs, and in a disagreement, neither of you are likely to back down or compromise.

What You Need to Know

You have numerous friends and acquaintances, and your social calendar is usually jammed. In a dating relationship with a Scorpio, this could be a problem. You don't want Scorpio to feel that she's being squeezed in between drinks and dinner. Be sure she knows how important she is to you. So instead of suggesting that the two of you join your thirty friends for dinner, have dinner just with her and then get together with those friends afterward.

Most of the time, you approach life with optimism and buoyancy and give other people the benefit of the doubt. You're a person for whom the glass is always full. Scorpio is more cautious, reserved, reticent—and suspicious. But for both of you, trust must be earned, and once it is, you and Scorpio can commit fully to the relationship and see where it goes!

A challenge with this combination is that you both have a tendency to believe you're right. This area is one that's perfect for compromise.

In the Bedroom

Once you and Scorpio have earned each other's trust, it won't be long before you hit the bedroom. And here, you are evenly matched. You're both passionate individuals for whom sex is a prolonged banquet, a delightful journey of the senses. But remember that for Scorpio, sex is also a form of communication, a way of getting to know who you are in the core of your being. There may not be a lot of pillow talk—that is, secrets exchanged, yearnings discovered—but your body will be worshipped as though you are sacred.

For you, the bedroom is often a turning point in a relationship. But don't expect that just because you and Scorpio are now lovers, it means you are exclusive. Don't assume anything. When in doubt, ask, discuss and talk about it. What are your respective expectations and hopes for this relationship? Do either of you know yet?

If you're still in the early stages of your relationship, then just go with the flow, Leo. Don't push for answers that Scorpio may not even have yet.

What to Avoid

Think, for a moment, of your own pet peeves. What pushes your buttons? Now take a look at this bulleted list of the big DON'Ts for a Scorpio. No one is saying you have to follow these, Leo, and no one is telling you to be something you aren't. Think of the list as tips for a smooth relationship with Scorpio.

> ➤ Don't make everything about you. Leos are sometimes accused of being overly concerned with themselves, that their world revolves around me, me, me. Part of this tendency is the result of a need to be recognized and applauded.
> ➤ Don't assume you know what makes Scorpio tick. You don't and probably never will. Instead, be observant and ask questions.
> ➤ Don't insist that it's your way or the highway. If possible, learn to give a little, to compromise.
> ➤ Don't pretend to feel something you don't. While it's true that many Leos are consummate actors, it's one thing to create a mood or a persona, but something else to express feelings you don't have.
> ➤ Don't be unfaithful. If the relationship becomes exclusive, keep it that way.
> ➤ Don't violate Scorpio's innate privacy.

What to Embrace

You do much better at embracing things than being told no. So post this list where you'll see it often. Embrace:

> ➤ Scorpio's esoteric interests. Our journey through life is about self-discovery and realizing our potential. In this regard, Scorpio can be an excellent teacher.

- Scorpio's gut feelings. Most of the time, Scorpio's hunches are correct. And when they aren't, it's usually because she didn't interpret them correctly.
- Sex with Scorpio.
- Scorpio's mystique. It's undoubtedly what attracted you to this person. Just understand that you may never crack the mystique wide open.
- Scorpio's creative talents. Depending on how this relationship evolves, your respective creative abilities may bond you completely.

Compatibility

One of the most famous Leo/Scorpio couples in the world is Bill and Hillary Clinton. They brought their respective strengths and passion for politics to the relationship and became a power couple.

Bill, the Leo, could have retired from public life after he left the White House, but instead he became a statesman. Hillary could have returned to the practice of law, but instead became a senator and ran for the presidency. The point is that they pursued their individual dreams, and despite scandals and endless media coverage, are still together.

This combination isn't the easiest, Leo. Know that from the outset. Fire and water signs have very different approaches to life. Fire signs are about action, movement, aggression and leadership. Water signs are about emotions, intuition and the inner reality. But the Leo/Scorpio combination can be one of the most creative and powerful.

Making Scorpio Happy

The next time you're at a bookstore, cruise through the self-help section. Many of the books are related to happiness—finding it, keeping it, defining it and explaining how you, too, can find happiness by following this or that author's advice. But ultimately, no one can teach you how to be happy and no one else can make you happy.

That said, there are things we can do for other people that bring them happiness. Scorpio is happiest when he's accepted as he is. So if you have criticisms, Leo, keep them to yourself. Scorpios generally enjoy research and investigating, and if you can facilitate that process in some way, he'll be delighted.

Honesty also makes Scorpio happy. He prefers being honest in a dating relationship and appreciates it when his partner is honest as well.

Advice for Scorpio

Fire signs are challenging for you, Scorpio. But there is so much passion and pizzazz in this relationship that you must practice what you preach and learn to bend and compromise for it to work.

Virgo Dating a Scorpio

Home, at last

Ah. This combination feels like a homecoming. You're attracted to
Scorpio's intensity, Virgo, to the inscrutable mystery so inherent in these
individuals. You may feel that if you can penetrate to the core of this
mystery, you'll discover something vital to your own being.

Your penchant for details, for connecting the dots, enables you to dig just
as deeply as Scorpio does into topics that interest you. In this sense, you
two really complement each other, and a dating relationship could easily
become a business partnership as well.

The challenges in this combination are actually small and stem from
Scorpio's inflexibility and your tendency to critique yourself and others.
It's not that you criticize just to criticize, but that you see yourself as a
diamond in the rough that must constantly be polished and perfected.
And this perfecting stuff often spills over into your personal environment.

What You Need to Know

As a Mercury-ruled earth sign, your intellect is razor sharp and you're
known for your mental agility and, often, acerbic wit. You tend to
attract people who are stimulating or eccentric in some way, and Scorpio
certainly fits the bill. But for you, like Gemini, the other sign ruled by
Mercury, there has to be a mental connection for a relationship to work,
an intellectual spark, a flow in your communication.

Scorpio may not be as forthcoming in the communication department
as you would like, but you can easily find your way around that. You're a
gifted conversationalist, and your skill with details will quickly uncover

Scorpio's passions and interests. Once you have that piece of the puzzle, you can determine whether the relationship interests you. Many of your decisions are made in this analytical, discriminating way, and romance is no exception.

For Scorpio, such decisions are usually made intuitively, and she may not even be able to verbalize why she is or isn't attracted to someone. For Scorpio, there are no shades of gray; for you, few things are black or white.

In the Bedroom
In romance, you can be flirtatious and coy, and Scorpio will love all that—to a point. And the point usually arrives when you're deciding whether to take the relationship to a more intimate level. You may have decided yes two days ago but now you're uncertain or maybe you've changed your mind altogether. This kind of waffling will drive Scorpio nuts. C'mon, Scorpio will be thinking. Yes or no, what's so difficult about that?

Once you've made the decision, though, you and Scorpio are in for a delightful surprise. Your analytical brain takes a vacation, you become pure sensation and Scorpio indulges you completely.

One-night stands probably don't interest you; so before the bedroom moment arrives you already know this won't happen just once. You'll already know that Scorpio won't be gone without good-byes in the morning. And Scorpio knows it, too. The two of you are on the same page in that you prefer relationships that evolve over time, with mutual interests and passions unfolding in a natural way.

What to Avoid
This list is short. You have a good sense about what turns a Scorpio off because many of the same behaviors and attributes turn you off. The thing you should be cautious about, Virgo, is that you can sometimes seem emotionally detached in a relationship. One moment, Scorpio sees you as open and talkative and the next moment, you're quiet and remote

and act like you couldn't care less. Scorpio will have to learn not to take it personally and you'll need to learn to temper this behavior.

Some Scorpios are controlling. If you find this to be so with the Scorpio you're dating, it's best to confront her and clear the air. Otherwise, it could become an issue in the relationship.

Here are a few others pointers:

> Don't be impatient. While it's true that some things in life don't move quickly enough to suit you, it's also true that you can never rush a Scorpio.
> Don't criticize Scorpio. Constructive criticism is fair, particularly if your dating relationship also involves work, but criticizing just to criticize will send Scorpio packing fast.
> Don't fret about tomorrow. Trust that your life is humming along just as it should.

What to Embrace

It won't take long to know what to embrace in this relationship with a Scorpio.

> Great conversation. You probably will have conversations and discussions with Scorpio that you won't have with people of other signs. The breadth of his interests may astonish you.
> Wonderful sex—once you've made up your mind!
> The enigma. This may seem like an oxymoron to you, Virgo, but part of Scorpio's appeal for you is that she's a paradox even to herself.
> The intense emotions. These intense emotions Scorpio experiences permeate everything she does, every choice she makes, every thought she thinks, every dream she has. Scorpio's emotions are the lens through which she views the world. If you can't embrace this, then the relationship won't work regardless of how otherwise compatible you are.

Compatibility

Both you and Scorpio enjoy rich inner lives and arrive at this place through different means. Your realm is that of ideas, and when you're really interested in something, you dive in with all the enthusiasm and energy you possess. The quest becomes part of your inner life. Scorpio's realm is that of feelings, of great sweeping contrasts, and at times, the quest may consume him completely.

Spiritually, you're well matched. It's likely that neither of you adheres to any traditional religious belief. You're both more interested in how you can evolve spiritually and creatively in this lifetime and you delve into the deeper mysteries—reincarnation, life after death, spirit communication, the paranormal, things that go bump in the night. This bond is powerful.

Making Scorpio Happy

You're balking at the subheading, right? So let's be clear right up front: it's not up to you to make Scorpio happy. But when Scorpio is happy in the relationship, you are, too. The reverse is also true. Honesty makes Scorpio happy. So does openness and integrity. You love your freedom every bit as much as Scorpio does, so give him room to indulge his interests and passions. And while you're at it, explore some of those mysteries with him, you know, like the ghost-hunting mystery or the afterlife mystery.

Advice for Scorpio

It's best to remember that Virgo needs to be appreciated, applauded, patted on the back. Express your feelings for her several times a day. Make it clear that you appreciate her and think she's special.

♎ + ♏
Libra Dating a Scorpio

Seductive & Romantic

Libras come in three distinct types: those who are decisive, those who aren't and those who seek harmony for its own sake. Like your air sign sibling, Gemini, you're all about ideas and the intellect, and have a natural love of beauty in all its forms. You seek to mediate and balance and use intelligence and diplomacy to get what you want. You're one of the true romantics of the zodiac, with refined tastes.

It's said that for a Libra, relationships are everything. Scorpio doesn't share that need, so that could be a potential conflict with this combination. But, like you, Scorpio flourishes in an enduring relationship, so let's take a deeper look at how this dating relationship might work.

What You Need to Know

Beneath your sociable, pleasant exterior lies the insight of a psychic. You're such an astute observer of people that when Scorpio's emotional intensity threatens to overwhelm you, you're able to sidestep it and then delve into it. For you, this intensity becomes an unexplored country, a geography to learn about, something to scrutinize from all angles so that you can understand it. You handle this intensity in the same way that you handle everything else in your life—with grace and equanimity.

Scorpio's need to investigate and research, to get to the absolute bottom line may not be your approach to life. But because it's a facet of the human mind, you're intrigued and fascinated by it and by Scorpio's persistence. You may even join Scorpio in some of these explorations to gain a better sense of how it all works.

Despite the differences with these two signs—air and water, cardinal and fixed—this combination can work well. The one area of possible conflict is that you may have to bend like a flower in the wind at times to accommodate Scorpio's stubbornness. Just be careful about always giving in.

In the Bedroom

You're a flirt, seductive and romantic, and that appeals to Scorpio's sensuous and passionate nature. You're comfortable with your sexuality and don't have any hard and fast rules about whether a relationship should be committed or not for the enjoyment of sex. That suits Scorpio, too. But before you take the relationship to a more intimate level, be sure it's what you want to do, particularly if you're an indecisive type of Libra. Any indecision on your part will squash things before you even reach the bedroom.

Bring your enjoyment of beauty and romance into the bedroom. Set the mood—freshly cut flowers, candlelight, an erotic scent or oil. Whether it's your first time together or not, setting a mood is a reflection of who you are, Libra, and Scorpio will appreciate the thoughtfulness that goes into it.

What you should remember about Scorpio is that sex is a way for her to get to know you in a different way. Through the rushing river of her passions and the penetrating insights of her intuition, she uncovers the deeper part of who you are. In a dating relationship, you are Scorpio's newest journey into the unknown.

What to Avoid

There are times when Scorpio's raw intensity may manifest itself in negative ways—jealousy, attempts to control you or others, sudden bursts of anger. These types of behaviors are a total turnoff for you; you're just looking for balance and harmony. So if you see these behaviors, back off. Avoid them altogether. A confrontation isn't worth the hassle.

We've all got pet peeves, and Scorpio is no exception. Here are some other pointers for maintaining harmony in a dating relationship with a Scorpio.

➤ Don't push Scorpio to do something he really doesn't want to do. If you would like to attend an opera or an art exhibit and he doesn't, find a friend to go with you.
➤ Don't expect Scorpio to adhere to your schedule.
➤ Don't give in all the time to Scorpio's wants and needs. He'll think you're a pushover.
➤ Don't expect Scorpio to like all your friends or to enjoy socializing with them every weekend. The reverse is also true!

What to Embrace

Once you know what to avoid in a dating relationship with a Scorpio, it's easy to know what to embrace about this sign:

➤ Fearlessness. This trait manifests itself in a variety of ways—from creative projects that may be risky to certain types of sports that Scorpio may enjoy.
➤ Persistence. Scorpio, like her fixed sign siblings Taurus and Leo, exhibits this trait continually in both her personal and professional lives.
➤ Intuition. Most Scorpios are deeply intuitive, and in some of them, the ability is so developed they are psychic.
➤ Creative ability. This sign's creative skills span the spectrum from the arts to the hard sciences. They are captivated by any creative pursuit that requires focus and research.
➤ Mastery of finance. Many Scorpios are masters at using other people's money and resources to build their own fortunes.

Compatibility

Thanks to your people skills, Libra, compatibility probably won't be an issue. You're famous for being able to get along with virtually anyone. But if compatibility is questionable, you probably will know early on, before you get attached to each other.

But if you are attached when you discover you aren't very compatible, then it's best to be up front about it, Libra. You sometimes stay in a relationship longer than you should because you dislike hurting anyone and find disharmony and confrontation so distasteful. But sticking around longer than you should only leads to secrecy, dishonesty and trouble.

Scorpio can be quite aggressive at times and that could be a deal breaker for you. On the other hand, if you compromise too much and too often just to keep Scorpio happy, that could be a deal breaker for him. This combination works best when one of you has the moon, Venus or Mars in the other's sun sign.

Making Scorpio Happy

No, it's not your job to make Scorpio happy. But there are things you can do that will light up her life:

- ➤ Setting a romantic mood
- ➤ Cooking something special. Some Libras are excellent cooks, and if you're one of them, go exotic!
- ➤ Talking about his esoteric interests

Advice for Scorpio

Indulge his interests in art and music. Open your heart to the beauty Libra brings into your life. Be appreciative.

♏ + ♏
Scorpio Dating a Scorpio

Powerhouse

In a science fiction novel, this combination could create and destroy worlds. In real life, the attraction feels magnetic, visceral, a kind of soul recognition. It's likely that you're both on the same page in terms of the important stuff—worldview, general beliefs, your approach to life.

But with this combination, the sign and position of your respective natal moons may be a determining factor in how the relationship evolves. The moon in astrology symbolizes your inner world, your capacity to nurture and be nurtured, your emotions and intuition. If your moon signs are compatible, then the relationship has the right potential for something enduring.

Look at the elements of your respective moon signs. If one of you has an earth sign moon—Taurus, Virgo or Capricorn—and the other has a water sign moon—Cancer, Scorpio or Pisces—then there's a powerful emotional flow between you that is also grounded in reality. Or, let's say one of you has an air sign moon—Gemini, Libra, Aquarius—and the other has a fire sign moon—Aries, Leo, Sagittarius. That combination would suggest intellectual compatibility and a similar approach to creative endeavors.

What You Need to Know

With this combination, the two of you cut to the chase rather quickly. You won't be circling each other warily for days or weeks, trying to figure each other out, establish boundaries or any of the other things people do when they date. You'll already have a strong intuitive sense of who the other person is. That initial point of attraction is the pivot on which the relationship turns and everything else shoots out from there, like spokes in a wheel.

A lot of what goes on in this relationship occurs on an intuitive, subliminal level. The vast oceans of your respective inner, emotional worlds come together in a way that may be difficult for either of you to verbalize. But you don't have to articulate this process in order to understand it. That's the beauty of the combination. You're like two beans in a pod, sharing this inner space in harmony with each other.

The one area of possible conflict centers on your respective inflexibility. Compromise is a foreign concept to both of you. This issue may crop up fairy quickly in the relationship and could be over something as simple as which movie to see or which TV show to watch. One or both of you will have to learn to bend a little.

In the Bedroom

Here's where it all should work beautifully. Romance, seduction, passion and emotional intensity: it's like *50 Shades of Grey* without the head games or the power plays. The plotline is straightforward, and the sensuality is a powerful river in which you both immerse yourselves.

Anything in the external world that hasn't been working between the two of you is left outside the bedroom door. This place is sacrosanct, and it's where your knowledge and understanding of each other should deepen. In fact, things in the bedroom may go so well that you just want to stay there!

The bedroom may be where important decisions are made about the relationship, about levels of commitment, whether or not you're exclusive. It's where you'll discover the essential core of who you are as a couple. Is it worth pursuing long-term? Is this relationship headed for marriage?

What to Avoid

For a couple of Scorpios in a dating relationship, this section is probably a no-brainer: avoid your own pet peeves.

- ➤ Don't assume that you know where the relationship stands unless you've talked about it.
- ➤ Don't put on airs or pretend to be something you're not. Scorpio will see through it immediately. It's unlikely that a Scorpio would do this to begin with. But if you have a fire sign moon, for instance, you might be more prone to this type of behavior.
- ➤ Don't lie. Scorpios usually have a lot of integrity, but if they're pushed into a corner, they may try to lie their way out.
- ➤ Don't insist that it's your way or the highway.
- ➤ Don't whine, complain or criticize. You know, after all, how these behaviors drive you nuts, so don't inflict them on another Scorpio.

What to Embrace

This section may also prove to be a no-brainer. What do you like best about yourself? What attributes do you admire in yourself? What are your strengths? See what I mean? You can probably create your own list of what to embrace. But here are some guidelines:

- ➤ Persistence. When Scorpio wants something, she won't take no for an answer. And it doesn't matter what it is—a relationship, a job, a goal or climbing to the top of Kilimanjaro.
- ➤ Emotionally intense romance. You may not always know where you stand in this relationship, so stay in the moment and allow yourself to be swept away.
- ➤ Sex. Relax and enjoy it.
- ➤ The intuitive connection. This bond may be exceptionally strong right from the beginning. You'll be thinking something, and Scorpio will voice it. You'll be thinking of her, and she'll call.

Compatibility

This combination is extremely compatible as long as you each understand the other's intensity, passions and gripes. But since no one understands Scorpio better than another Scorpio, isn't it a relief that you don't have to get past that barrier?

You two engage in this relationship with a finely attuned sonar that detects most obstacles and barriers before you reach them. This sonar enables you to find your way around anything that might impede your personal and collective growth—creatively, spiritually, romantically—and as long as you maintain this uniquely Scorpio equilibrium, the relationship flourishes.

This sonar may even enable you to learn how to compromise. Start with small things—what TV show you'll watch, which movie you'll go to or where you'll eat. As you learn to compromise with these small things, you'll be much better equipped to deal with the larger issues, if and when they surface.

Making Scorpio Happy

Another no-brainer. What makes you happiest, Scorpio? Digging through ruins in some far-flung part of the world? Researching an ancient mystery? Getting lost in a transformative novel or movie? Walking barefoot on a beach? Jogging three miles? Enjoying a delicious home-cooked meal? Delving into a creative project?

Follow your intuition. It won't fail you!

Advice for the Other Scorpio

Think about what pushes your buttons and then avoid those behaviors with your partner. This one is really a no-brainer. What you like, she'll like. What makes you crazy will probably be the same things that make her crazy.

Sagittarius Dating a Scorpio

A Zinger!

Fire and water. Back to basic chemistry. Let's see how this combination could work.

You, Sagittarius, are the nomad of the zodiac. For some of you, it's actual physical travel that takes you to exotic ports of call where you immerse yourself in a foreign culture. For other Sadges, the travel is mental and whisks you off to worlds you create in your head, in your imagination. But always, you're after the truth, whatever it might be, and your quest concerns the larger picture, how things fit together and why. And this is the place where you and Scorpio connect.

Scorpio's quest is finding the absolute bottom line, the what, how, where and why of anything he tackles. It doesn't matter whether it's a relationship, idea, creative project, business deal or house hunt, Scorpio's piercing insight drills through the complexities. Your quest for the truth works in much the same way but moves outward instead of inward, through connecting with people, by getting out and about and taking action.

What You Need to Know

You value your freedom every bit as much as Scorpio values her independence. In fact, those two words, freedom and independence, may be interchangeable in this dating relationship.

However, Scorpio may be initially put off by your bluntness, by your natural inclination to call things as you see them. It may catch Scorpio off-guard. Just when she's expecting some superficial, amusing remark, you come out with some sharply honest observation that leaves her speechless. She comes to appreciate this about you.

By the same token, you may find Scorpio's reticence irritating. You enjoy discussion—about anything and everything. When it comes to talking about what you feel, particularly in a relationship, it could end up as a one-way conversation.

In terms of spirituality and the psychic realms, you and Scorpio are probably well matched. You sample a vast array of spiritual traditions and may travel in your spiritual explorations. Scorpio is also a sampler, but for her, it's more of an internal process and exploration, an intuitive journey. You can be quite prescient at times, and if you combine that vision with Scorpio's intuition, there is no telling what the two of you might foresee.

In the Bedroom

Ah, here's where the truth comes out. You're a natural flirt and your warmth and sensuality are such an intimate part of you that you couldn't disguise or hide these qualities even if you wanted to. In an uncommitted relationship, you're looking for fun and diversion, variety and excitement, and your need for freedom keeps you free of emotional entanglements. You aren't the jealous or possessive type and are fairly casual about sex.

This casualness changes when you find a partner who ignites your imagination, shares at least some of your passions, and who gives you the freedom you demand. Then sex becomes a way to communicate and to connect at a spiritual and psychic level. And this is where you and Scorpio excel together. Once the relationship is sexually exclusive, your and Scorpio's capacity for intimacy is practically infinite.

What to Avoid

Sagittarius generally doesn't take well to rules and regulations, to lists of DOs and DON'Ts. But if you see sufficient promise in your relationship with Scorpio, there are simple behaviors you can avoid to keep things running smoothly.

- ➢ Don't assume that because you believe something, Scorpio does too. Scorpio feels his way through life. You are driven to act. That's one of the primary differences between fire and water signs.
- ➢ Don't shove your friends into Scorpio's life. Your network of friends and acquaintances is undoubtedly vast, but unless Scorpio has a sociable air or fire sign moon, he may not appreciate spending an evening sharing you with your friends.
- ➢ Don't take Scorpio for granted. He won't like it any more than you do!
- ➢ Don't surrender your autonomy. Such surrender is unlikely for a Sagittarius, but if you succumb, it would be an invitation for Scorpio to control you. And then the relationship would end quickly.

What to Embrace

This list will be right up your alley, Sagittarius, and some of these attributes will be obvious to you early on in your dating relationship.

- ➢ Scorpio's piercing insights. Her hunches are often correct and when they aren't, it's because her left brain intervened. The same is probably true for you and your hunches, Sadge.
- ➢ Scorpio's sexual intensity and passion
- ➢ Scorpio's resilience. The word "obstacle" doesn't exist in Scorpio's vocabulary. When Scorpio encounters what would be an impenetrable wall to someone else, he simply finds a way around it.

Compatibility

You're compatible, but with caveats. If you and Scorpio disagree on something, she's incredibly stubborn about changing her mind, belief or opinion, and you may have to simply agree to disagree. That sounds reasonable, right? But if the disagreement concerns something about which you feel passionate—war, animals' rights, a woman's right to choose, issues about personal freedoms—agreeing to disagree may not be an option for you.

You're most compatible when you're engaged in activities or exploring interests that you have in common. Find the commonalities and capitalize on them.

Making Scorpio Happy

Scorpio wants to trust you; she really does. And she's happiest when you've proven that you're trustworthy. Of course, you're not on the planet to make Scorpio or anyone else happy, but in this relationship, the actual parameters are straightforward. If you and Scorpio decide your relationship is sexually exclusive, then be sure to abide by that agreement. If you don't want an exclusive relationship, then let Scorpio know up front.

That's the whole thing, really. Scorpio wants to love and be loved, in a relationship that isn't duplicitous, where she and her partner are supportive of each other.

Advice for Scorpio

Travel with Sadge. It will be an experience you won't ever forget, and Sadge will appreciate your willingness to join her.

Capricorn Dating a Scorpio

Smooth Sailing

Earth and water. This one feels like home, doesn't it? You and Scorpio share more similarities than you do differences, so the bottom line provides a much firmer base on which to build a relationship than some of the other combinations.

You're both rather serious people, but you tend to be more aloof and in control of your emotions. You're more easily impressed by outward signs of success but are less interested in money than you are in the power that money represents. Like Scorpio, you feel the need to rule whatever kingdom you occupy—home, workplace, business or a relationship. And this could be a potential challenge in the relationship.

You are both industrious individuals. You, in particular, Capricorn, are efficient and disciplined, able to work out practical ways of attaining your goals. Scorpio's approach is more intuitive, but your different methods take you to the same place.

What You Need to Know

You may feel overwhelmed at times by Scorpio's emotional intensity, but once you understand its origins, you're able to accommodate it. Truth is, Capricorn, you're pretty intense yourself at times, especially when you're focused on a singular goal. Scorpio may find you something of an enigma, a real oxymoron since to most people Scorpio is an enigma. When two enigmas begin dating, the puzzle of who they are is solved through careful observation and patience.

Both of you dislike wasting time and aren't frivolous in your affections. You both have a clear sense of what you're looking for in a partner, and if you don't see those qualities quickly, that's it. The relationship is over, and you both move on.

In the Bedroom

For you, sex is an adventure—and yet, you aren't into casual affairs. You're after genuine commitment, a genuine partner, and when you find such a person, you're faithful and loving. So, with Scorpio, you probably won't leap into the bedroom on the first date. Or the thirtieth date. It will happen only when you're as sure as you can be that the relationship is worth pursuing. That said, it's also true that when you are viscerally attracted to someone, the bedroom may be one of your first stops, if only to prove to yourself that the chemistry is real.

All of this suits Scorpio, who doesn't need commitment for an intimate relationship but often prefers it. In the bedroom, you both come to realize that you have similar expectations, needs and desires. The focused determination that is so prevalent for both of you in daily life falls away in the bedroom, and you become explorers—sometimes serious, sometimes lighthearted, and forever curious about what may be discovered in the next moment and the next.

What to Avoid

The basic compatibility with these two signs is so strong that there really isn't much to avoid. However, if we're going to nitpick, here are some guidelines:

- ➤ Don't bring your work concerns to the dating relationship—unless you and Scorpio are also business/creative partners.
- ➤ Don't agree to something and then back down. Even though ambivalence is rare for a Capricorn, it will drive Scorpio nuts.
- ➤ Don't insist on defining the relationship. It will define itself early on.

What to Embrace

There's no shortage of things to embrace in this relationship and many of them will be quickly obvious.

- ➤ Smoldering sexuality. This may trigger your visceral attraction to Scorpio. You'll feel compelled to find out what's really behind those intense, penetrating eyes, that quick smile and that intriguing conversation.
- ➤ Intuitive guidance. Scorpio's intuition often borders on clairvoyance, and you'll see evidence of it in this relationship.
- ➤ Persistence. You have this quality as well, Capricorn, and when you and Scorpio join forces in this regard, you're unstoppable.

Compatibility

You're the builder of the zodiac, the architect who envisions a goal and goes after it. You lay down a strategy and fine-tune it as you move forward. Like Scorpio, you refuse to acknowledge obstacles. When you come up against something immovable, you find a way around it and, always, your eyes are on the summit. You don't do anything halfway. You don't begin something and then abandon it before it's attained or achieved. Neither does Scorpio. In a dating relationship, you and Scorpio may discover that you're quite formidable as a duo.

Your compatibility is without question. But, as the saying goes, the devil may lie in the details. So as this relationship evolves, pay attention to the details, the small gestures and the minutiae. Take nothing for granted.

Making Scorpio Happy

What makes you the happiest in a relationship, Capricorn? Make a list. Then ask Scorpio to do the same thing. Compare your lists. Chances are you'll discover you've jotted down many of the same things.

- ➢ Not being taken for granted
- ➢ Appreciation for who I am
- ➢ Honesty
- ➢ Laughter
- ➢ A relationship that is balanced, without drama
- ➢ Common interests
- ➢ Independence

Advice for Scorpio

Never underestimate Capricorn or take her for granted. These two things alone will ensure a smooth sail!

Aquarius Dating a Scorpio

Unpredictable

As the non-conformist of the zodiac, Aquarius, you're an original thinker who refuses to accept something as true just because someone else tells you so. You have to find out on your own what is true or not true, real or not real. In this way your life is like a Zen koan. What is the sound of one hand clapping? You may not have that answer today, but you're determined to find it even if it takes several lifetimes. And this persistence, this tenacity, the fixed quality of both signs, is what you and Scorpio have in common.

The scope and breadth of Scorpio's knowledge and insight will provide plenty of fodder for seducing you intellectually. Once that happens, your attraction to Scorpio deepens considerably.

An area of possible conflict revolves around the fixed natured of your respective signs. You're both stubborn, slow to change your opinions and beliefs and compromise is a foreign concept. In a disagreement, neither of you is likely to compromise.

What You Need to Know

Scorpio's emotional intensity is directly contrary to your emotional detachment and may be one of the reasons this relationship begins as a friendship. For you, friendship is an integral part of the success of any dating relationship. It gives you a chance to get to know Scorpio first as an individual, and you're both free of expectations.

Once the friendship morphs into a dating relationship, though, you demand a great deal of freedom to pursue your own path and Scorpio welcomes it. Her independence is vital to her well-being, too. Separate but equal, together and equal. The caveat with this equation is that if you are both so intent on pursuing your own paths, the relationship may take a back seat to everything else.

In the Bedroom

You rarely have any compunction about initiating sex, but sex actually interests you less than establishing a meaningful connection and a foundation of trust that facilitates communication. Scorpio feels much the same way about sex, but for her it's also a way to understand you more deeply.

Until you have established trust between yourself and Scorpio, you won't be eager to establish parameters about exclusivity or to talk about where the relationship is going. Once that trust is established, though, you're a faithful, loving partner with a tremendous capacity for intimacy. Secrets will be shared, histories will be exchanged and you'll be on your way toward enjoying a relationship filled with peak moments.

What to Avoid

Think of things other people do that drive you absolutely nuts. Chances are many of those pet peeves are also on Scorpio's list. In order to enjoy a harmonious relationship with Scorpio, keep these bulleted points in mind:

➢ Don't assume anything about Scorpio. Within the complex labyrinth of his emotions, there are places you will never touch, shadows you'll never pierce. If you try to second-guess him, you probably will guess wrong.

➢ Don't doubt your own hunches just because Scorpio believes you're wrong. Even though his intuitive insights are powerful, they aren't always right! And if you begin doubting yourself, it will only compound challenges in your life.

➢ Don't lie. It's unlikely that you'll lie even to save face. You value honesty too much to compromise yourself that way. But if you're tempted with a "white lie," back off.

➢ Don't thrust Scorpio into a group of your diverse friends without a little warning. Your friends are probably as eccentric as you are, and even Scorpio could feel a bit overwhelmed.

What to Embrace

There's a lot to embrace in this relationship and it begins with communication. Because Scorpio is forever looking for the absolute bottom line, the range of his interests captivates you. Your muse is engaged. Your innate visionary ability is triggered. Your sexuality flourishes. In case that's not enough to embrace, here's more:

> Freedom. Scorpio gives you all the freedom you could possibly need or want to pursue your own interests and friendships.
> Compassion. As a water sign who feels her way through life, Scorpio's compassion for others is a powerful motivating force for impacting lives in a positive way.
> Creativity. Many Scorpios have unusual creative abilities. This appeals to you in a visceral way and could be combined with an ability you have to create something truly unique.

Compatibility

Once you and Scorpio discover the interests and passions you have in common and understand each other's respective need for freedom and independence, this relationship works well. But getting to this point can be challenging.

Air and water signs have distinctly different approaches to life and living. Air signs are mental, active and social. Their lives are outer-directed. Water signs are emotional and intuitive, and their lives are inner-directed. These tendencies can challenge or serve as a balance. It depends on how willing you and Scorpio are to integrate your differences into the relationship.

Making Scorpio Happy

Just to be clear: you aren't here to make Scorpio happy. The reverse is also true. But in a relationship, there are things you can do that will light up Scorpio's life:

> Bring Scorpio a special gift, something you know he or she will love. It doesn't have to be expensive. It's the thought behind it that counts.
> Cook a meal of Scorpio's favorite food, whatever that might be.
> Surprise Scorpio with something—a trip, a psychic reading, a book or a movie.
> Compliment Scorpio in the same way that you like to be complimented.

Simple, right?

Advice for Scorpio

Share your explorations into the unknown and the mysterious. Do research on-site. Aquarius loves a quest just as much as you do, and such adventures will cement the bond.

Pisces Dating a Scorpio

Mystical

You, Pisces, like Scorpio, explore the world through your emotions and intuition. You swim through seas of impressions that would exhaust lesser human beings. You feel things so deeply at times that you become a kind of psychic sponge that absorbs the emotions of the people around you. It's why it's so important for you to surround yourself with positive individuals.

You and your mutable sibling, Gemini, are the only signs represented by two of something—for you, it's two fish, swimming in opposite directions. The fish symbolize your head and your heart, or your ego and your soul. One shouts at you to go in this direction; the other demands to go in the other direction. As a result, you're sometimes torn between the two and become indecisive, a quality that will drive Scorpio batty. That said, you two have quite a bit in common.

What You Need to Know

You and Scorpio both need time alone, but for different reasons. Solitude enables you to detach from the emotions of the people around you so that you can center yourself. Without this solitude, it becomes increasingly difficult for you to sort out what you feel and what other people feel. You then become moody and withdrawn.

For Scorpio, solitude is as necessary as breathing, a time to delve into her own creativity, to investigate and explore the unseen and the unknown. It's also the time she uses to understand herself and the complex emotions that drive her. If you can manage to be alone together, then this combination may have all the makings of an ideal relationship.

For both of you, loving and being loved is essential to happiness. You're more romantic than Scorpio is, but with some gentle nudging Scorpio will get the idea! For you, romance and love can become a point of transcendence, enabling you to penetrate the larger mysteries that fascinate you. For Scorpio, this point of transcendence is his sexuality.

In the Bedroom

Your sensuality and Scorpio's sexuality are a terrific combination in the bedroom, particularly once Scorpio understands just how much you enjoy romance. The dance of seduction, the mood and the setting all enhance your experience. Sex is another form of creative expression for you, and just about anything goes.

Where sex for Scorpio is about learning who you are in the most private pockets of your soul, you're looking for a connection to soul. It may or may not be there with Scorpio, but one thing is for sure: pleasure lies in the exploration and discovery.

It's undoubtedly wise to establish early on whether the relationship is exclusive. Your feelings are easily hurt, and if you just assume exclusivity and then find out otherwise, trust issues will surface and the relationship will be forever sullied for you. By the same token, if you have assumed the relationship is non-exclusive, and Scorpio had been led to believe otherwise and finds out different after the fact, it won't just be hurt feelings. He'll walk.

What to Avoid

You aren't being asked to change your personality or your approach to life. But if you want to enjoy a harmonious relationship with Scorpio, here's a bullet list of things to avoid.

> ➤ Don't say you'll be at a particular place at a particular time or that you're going to do something and then change your mind. Ambivalence and indecisiveness aren't in Scorpio's vocabulary.
> ➤ Don't adapt a point of view just to please Scorpio. She'll think you're a pushover.
> ➤ Don't sacrifice your solitude to meet Scorpio's schedule.
> ➤ Don't distance yourself from your friends if Scorpio doesn't like them.
> ➤ Don't allow Scorpio's intensity to overwhelm you. Simply detach from the situation and do something else.

What to Embrace

This one is easy!

> ➤ Sex and sensuality
> ➤ Invigorating conversation
> ➤ Spiritual and intuitive connection
> ➤ Creativity

Compatibility

The compatibility factors are favorable, as long as you both adhere to certain parameters and respect your personal boundaries. The planets that rule your respective signs have a lot to say about what you have in common and your differences.

Pisces is ruled by elusive Neptune, the planet often referred to as the higher octave of Venus. It's co-ruled by expansive Jupiter. Scorpio is ruled by transformative Pluto and co-ruled by aggressive Mars. You're a dreamer who thinks big; Scorpio's innate curiosity and suspicion of easy answers compels him to probe deeply into whatever interests him. The relationship bridges these two approaches and, with a bit of effort, you and Scorpio can easily integrate your respective strengths.

Making Scorpio Happy

Scorpio needs independence and the freedom to pursue his passions and interests. But he's happiest when he knows he's loved and appreciated and that the relationship is built on trust. Central to the relationship for him is sex as a means for transcendence.

Advice for Scorpio

Pisces, like Cancer, is a gentle sign that dislikes drama and disagreement. Keep things simple and straightforward, Scorpio. If you find fault with Pisces, look within first to see if the fault actually lies in you.

Chapter 3:

Tying the Knot with a Scorpio

*"The thing women have yet to learn is nobody gives you power.
You just take it."*
Roseanne Barr, November 3

*"Do you seriously expect me to be the first Prince of Wales in history
not to have a mistress?"*
Charles, Prince of Wales, November 4

Marriage is a journey. At every step, you and your spouse discover something new about each other, something you may not have noticed when you were dating. When you're married to a Scorpio, this process of discovery is like peeling through the layers of the proverbial onion. The deeper you go into the onion, the closer you get to unlocking the secret of Scorpio. But what, exactly, is this secret? Even Scorpio can't answer that. But it's there, somewhere within, a diamond waiting to be unearthed, and the excavation occurs a step at a time, through the context of your daily lives together.

Let's take a deeper look at the details.

If you're fortunate enough to be married to a Scorpio woman,
understand that she has her own life, job, friends, career, goals and dreams, and the marriage will be integrated into all of it. If you lived together before tying the knot, then you already have a clear idea about the division of household chores, whether your finances will be separate or combined, about work hours, sleeping habits and all the rest of it. If you didn't live together, these things will find their natural flow.

That said, you'll find that the marriage relationship works best when you don't assume anything about the division of household labor. It's best to verbalize it right from the start, who does what. If you're the better cook, then you cook, and she'll clean up. Or vice versa.

She's accustomed to spending her money the way she wants and, depending on her income, may not be keen on combining financial resources. You may have to come up with a plan where each of you contributes a certain amount toward rent/mortgage, food and other shared expenses. Once you have been married for a while and trust about money has been established—i.e., she knows you're not going to run off with her bank account!—combined financial resources won't be an issue.

Capitalize on your respective skills and strengths.

When you're married to a Scorpio man, it's important to remember that he doesn't park his passions at the door when he gets married, so sometimes you may feel as if you're living with a crowd—his books, journals, sports equipment and the other stuff that's important to him. Everything he owns holds meaning and significance for him. He doesn't acquire just to own more.

He's usually careful with money and has a gift for investing. If you combine incomes, you may want to talk about setting aside a particular amount each month for investing in something that will pay dividends. He's a master at using other people's money to build your combined fortune.

Your spirituality as a married couple will develop with time. Some Scorpio men—and women—take to organized religion like the proverbial duck to water. Others, though, dive into unorthodox belief systems in search of spiritual answers. Whatever form your mutual spirituality takes, the search is rich with passion and sincerity. Just don't ever use that spirituality as an excuse to criticize him.

Aries Married to a Scorpio

An Adventure

In a marriage, this combination can be challenging. It's one thing to see each other once or twice a week, when it's all exciting and passionate and fun. But it's something else to live with each other on a daily basis. Your impatience, Aries, and Scorpio's penchant for secrecy and privacy may grate on each other, creating tension and disagreement. Through the ups and downs, your marriage will be an adventure that will continue to thrill and excite you both.

The ruling planets of your respective signs have a lot to say about this combination and why it can work—or not. Mars, which symbolizes our physical energy, sex drive, capacity for aggression, the way we pursue what we desire, rules Aries. Pluto, symbolic of how we transform and regenerate lives, rules Scorpio. But back before Pluto's discovery in 1930, Mars ruled Scorpio and is now it's co-ruler. And this is where you and Aries can connect. You both relentlessly pursue what you desire, are athletic and your sexuality is a central feature of your lives. In order to have a harmonious marriage in which you both have the opportunity to evolve and fulfill your potential on all levels, it's necessary to understand the areas that may be hot spots. Once you understand them, you can take steps to avoid conflict.

Hot Spots

Joint Finances. This area is touchy for a lot of married couples, not just Aries and Scorpio. But for you two, the resolution of the issue depends on the emotional baggage you're both bringing to the marriage, your respective beliefs about money and how willing you are to compromise. You, Aries, tend to be a bigger spender than Scorpio.

Domestic Stuff. If you've ever watched some of the old sitcoms from the 1960s—*Father Knows Best* and *The Donna Reed Show* are two that come immediately to mind—you're probably appalled by how black-and-white the roles were for men and women. The men went out into the world and made the money, the ladies stayed home and took care of the house and kids and all the domestic stuff. There was no discussion about it. It's just how things worked.

For Aries and Scorpio, it's best to have this issue resolved early on. Know who is going to do what and try to capitalize on your respective strengths. Don't argue about it. Just agree.

Career. If you both have careers, then have a clear understanding of each other's workloads, schedules and responsibilities. If Scorpio has to work on Saturdays, don't expect her to call in sick in order to go rock climbing with you. Or if you have to bring work home with you, Aries, don't expect Scorpio to sit around and watch you work!

Social Life. One of you may be more outgoing and social than the other and that's fine. Just be considerate of each other. If Scorpio is working on a major project, don't toss an informal party and invite twenty friends to your place. Or if you're immersed in something that requires concentration and focus, then Scorpio should watch football on a TV at the other end of the house.

Kids. Before you start a family, clarify how you would like to raise your children and who will do what. These things will undoubtedly change once the child arrives and will be different for each stage of the child's life, so be flexible!

If you have children, be sure to set aside time for your relationship. All too often, it's easy to get wrapped up in parenting, and the relationship goes on automatic.

Comfort Zones

Some parts of the marriage between Aries and Scorpio zip along at a pace that suits you both. Nurture these areas and everything else will go more smoothly:

Sex. You're both passionate people and intimacy is vital to the health of your marriage. Guard against bringing anger, resentment or jealousy into the bedroom with you. You want to keep your passions upbeat!

Physical Fitness. Sports and physical exercise are important to both of you. Find an activity the two of you can do together, and make it part of your regular routine.

Exploration. Whether it's exploring ancient ruins or searching for the truth about ancient aliens, you're both adventurous, fearless individuals who enjoy tackling what other people won't touch. But if you and Scorpio begin a quest together, make sure you see it through to the end, Aries. Don't start what you can't finish.

Creativity. By combining your creative talents, you create or achieve something that is uniquely yours. Whether it's a screenplay or a work of art, a decorating project or a garden, your connection to each other is strengthened considerably.

Tips

Here are some additional tips to keep your and Scorpio's marriage harmonious:

➢ Don't rush Scorpio. This one may be tough for you, Aries. You're usually in a hurry. If Scorpio can't keep pace with you and your timetable, disengage and call a friend who can.

➢ Stand up to Scorpio if she's making a power play or trying to control or manipulate you. It's unlikely that you allow yourself to be pushed around, but in the event that Scorpio attempts to do so, set her straight immediately. And Scorpio, if Aries is trying to push you around, stand up to him immediately.

➢ When you're in the midst of a meltdown, remind yourself why you married this person.

Unlocking the Secret to Scorpio

As a cardinal fire sign, the best way to unlock the secret to the person you married is through your pioneering spirit. Invite your spouse on your adventures, Aries. Include him in whatever you enjoy doing on the spur of the moment, on impulse. You'll see new facets of his personality open up. Or if you're involved in a creative project, invite him to contribute ideas or suggestions. This sort of creative exchange enables him to use his powerful intuition in a new way.

Famous Aries/Scorpio Couples

Rhea Perlman (Aries) and Danny DeVito (Scorpio)

Adam Shulman (Aries) and Anne Hathaway (Scorpio)

Elton John (Aries) and David Furnish (Scorpio)

Taurus Married to a Scorpio

Great Balance

Opposites attract. In a committed relationship like marriage, the "opposite" part of the equation often acts like a fulcrum, a perfect balance of strengths and weaknesses.

Taurus is ruled by Venus and Scorpio by Pluto and co-ruled by Mars. The rulers of your respective signs tell us quite a bit about how you each approach life in a marriage. You, Taurus, enjoy beautiful surroundings, music and art and are usually the one who enhances your home with nice things. You probably have a green thumb, too, and transform your yard or property with gorgeous flowers and trees. Scorpio appreciates the beauty, even revels in it when it's there, but can live with or without it.

For the most part, this marriage is harmonious. But when it's not, there are certain hot spots where the disagreements crop up. By being aware of what they are, you can take steps to mitigate them.

Hot Spots

Joint Finances. If you enter marriage with the attitude that *what's mine is mine and what's yours is yours,* the marriage may be off to a bumpy start. It's best to lay out the financial parameters before you tie the knot. If you choose to keep your finances separate, then you'll have to agree on who will pay what of the monthly expenses, which can get tricky if one of you loses or changes jobs. It's easier to simply pool your money, and then use your respective strengths to increase it.

You, Taurus, are a whiz at taking care of your daily finances and Scorpio excels at investments. You're adept with all the technology that enables you to make deposits and withdrawals electronically and are comfortable with various kinds of accounting software. Scorpio keeps track of stock prices, intuitively knows when to buy and sell and has an excellent grasp about how to increase your financial worth.

Domestic Stuff. The smart thing to do is to divide things up according to your strengths and skills. Many Tauruses are excellent cooks, so if you're going to do the bulk of the cooking, then Scorpio should do the cleanup. If you do most of the yard work, then Scorpio should do most of the house stuff. That's the fair way to do it. But what's fair in theory doesn't always work out in daily life, and that's when disagreements surface.

Presumably, you both have jobs/careers and may not always have enough time to do your share. If you can afford it, hire someone to clean your house and do your yard work. This area may become particularly muddled if children enter the picture, so it's best to spell things out early on.

Career. You are both hard workers, disciplined and relentless when it comes to your careers. No need to explain it to each other. The only way this area could become a hot spot is if one of you is self-employed and works from home and ends up doing most of the domestic stuff because of it.

Social Life. Both you and Scorpio tend to be solitary people rather than social butterflies who constantly surround themselves with friends and acquaintances. You have your separate friends and friends with whom you do things together. You have stuff you do separately. This area isn't likely to be much of a hot spot for either of you.

Kids. Children change the dynamics in most marriages. You and Scorpio have an advantage in that it's unlikely you'll get hung up on gender roles. If you, for instance, are a male Taurus but the more nurturing individual, then you may be the one who tends to the child's daily needs.

The one possible glitch—a potential hot spot—is if one of you is traditionally religious and the other isn't. In which spiritual tradition will the child be raised? Since neither of you is known for your ability to compromise, this could be a real stickler. A solution that might work? Raise the child by exposing her to both traditions.

Comfort Zones

You and Scorpio can probably spend hours together without feeling a need to converse every few minutes. You're both comfortable with silence, and besides, a lot of your communication takes place telepathically. One of you, for example, might be thinking about how great it would be to get out of town for the weekend and suddenly, the other says, "Hey, how about if we go somewhere this weekend?"

When this kind of communication occurs, you know your marriage is right where it should be, in the flow, the groove. This kind of synchronicity suggests that beneath the seemingly random nature of life, there's a deeper order, a quantum order, and you and Scorpio are tapped into it. Here are some other Comfort Zones you and Scorpio will enjoy:

Sex. Okay, so can there ever be too much of a good thing when it comes to sex? The answer from you both is a resounding NO! You, Taurus, are generally a more sensuous person than Scorpio, but in the bedroom Scorpio's sensuality can be breathtaking, particularly when she knows what you enjoy. So don't hold back. Let her know what really turns you on. And Scorpio should do the same. The stronger your sexual bond, the greater your intimacy and the stronger your marriage. It's like a mathematical axiom.

Physical Fitness. For many Tauruses, physical exercise is a sensuous experience and many of you have a regular routine that is part of your life—yoga, the gym, mountain biking, jogging. Exercise makes you acutely aware of your physical body. For many Scorpios, physical fitness is more about burning off that emotional intensity and staying fit. Exercise grounds them within their bodies. You're evenly matched on this score and may even be competitive on some level.

Travel. Not all Tauruses and Scorpios enjoy travel. But if you and your partner are among those who do, then the more exotic the locale, the happier you are. Your senses are fully engaged; your intuition is deepened. There may be some sort of quest involved in your travel, something the two of you hope to investigate and uncover.

The Mysterious & Inexplicable. Both you and Scorpio are often driven by a need to understand the nature of reality. The hidden side of life, the truth that lies in the shadows and in the inexplicable, fascinates and intrigues you, and its exploration is part of your journey together.

Tips

If you and Scorpio have known each other longer than five minutes, then most of these tips about maintaining harmony in your marriage will be obvious. If so, then consider this list a reminder.

➢ Compromise. Yes, this is difficult for a pair of fixed signs, but necessary in a marriage. And it shouldn't always be the same one of you who gives in. Take turns. Learn what you can live with.

➢ Nurture that telepathic communion you two share.

➢ Never neglect your sex life.

Unlocking the Secret to Scorpio

Persistence is your ally in unlocking the secret to Scorpio. Your excavation of the psyche of your spouse's personality, her consciousness, can't be rushed, and, perhaps, can't even be defined. But your patience is the key to the whole process.

Famous Taurus/Scorpio Couples

Al Pacino (Taurus) and Beverly D'Angelo (Scorpio)

Jessica Lange (Taurus) and Sam Shepard (Scorpio)

♊ + ♏
Gemini Married to a Scorpio

Guessing Game

Oops. Who did I marry? Now what? This may be how you felt, Gemini, the first day of your marriage to Scorpio.

And Scorpio, that first morning as you woke up, you probably thought, *Uh-oh, which twin did I marry?*

And that's the thing with this marriage combination. You keep each other guessing. Gemini, your sign is ruled by Mercury, the messenger—the planet that symbolizes communication, mental quickness and verbal acuity. The image for your sign is that of the twins, and it means you are often at odds with yourself. This internal conflict can manifest itself as two different people. No wonder Scorpio is wondering whom he married.

Scorpio, ruled by Pluto and co-ruled by Mars, tends to be inwardly focused on the things that interest him, so he may come across as remote. This, in turn, results in your moodiness, as discussed in the dating chapter. However, the place you two meet and commune is in the exploration of spiritual and psychic realms. It's where the single burning question of Gemini's life—why?—can be answered. And this place is the home of Scorpio's soul. But getting to this place in the marriage may be challenging. It helps if one or both of you have a moon or rising in the other's sign.

Hot Spots

These areas are just potential hot spots, and each combination of signs deals with them differently.

Joint Finances. How you handle money depends on which twin is in charge of the purse strings—the spendthrift or the saver? Either way, you probably aren't too concerned about combining your financial resources now that you're married. It strikes you as the logical thing to do, just as it seems logical to file a joint tax return. If the spendthrift twin is in charge, though, Scorpio may take exception to combining finances. It's smart to discuss this before wedding vows are uttered.

Domestic Stuff. Whether you're male or female, Gemini, you avoid domestic stuff. Yes, yes, you know someone has to cook meals, vacuum the cars, sweep, mop the floors, mow the grass and trim the hedges before they overtake your neighbor's yard. But it isn't going to be you. You're too busy earning a living, networking, reading books, going to movies or to the theater…you know, just living your life!

That worked when you were single—but it won't work at all now that you're married. If you leave all the domestic chores to Scorpio, you can be sure of one thing: you won't be married long. If Scorpio has rigid ideas about gender roles, then here's another certainty: you won't stick around. So this is an area where you should discuss and agree long before your home—and your marriage—descends into chaos!

Career. You and Scorpio have your own careers, professional goals and dreams about what you would like to achieve in the time you spend on the planet in this incarnation. You're both ambitious. The challenge here is to give your marriage relationship the time it deserves, and that might entail taking time off now and then to do whatever it is you enjoy doing together. Whether it's just hanging out at home or hitting the open road together for some sort of adventure, this time together should confirm why you married each other.

Social Life. This area could be a problem. You're very much a networker, with a zillion friends, some of them as close as your backyard, and others who are scattered across the planet. You stay in touch, too, through Skype, email, phone calls, texting, lunches, drinks, dinner or an impromptu party at your place.

Scorpio is more circumspect when it comes to friends and her social life. She probably has several really close friends and may not want to spend time with some of your friends and acquaintances. She definitely won't appreciate an impromptu party, particularly if you haven't mentioned it to her beforehand. So, Gemini, this is the place where you and Scorpio must set up boundaries. How you do this will depend on your respective priorities. What's most important in your life? Once you answer that question, you're on a path toward resolution.

Kids. When a family of two becomes a family of three or four or more, everything changes, all bets are off and boundaries and parameters are redrawn. Ideally, your parenting styles will reflect your strengths.

From you, your children will learn to love learning; from Scorpio, they will learn to never settle for easy answers. From you, they will learn the value of logic, reasoning and inquisitiveness; from Scorpio, they will learn the value of intuition and the power of emotions to move mountains. From both of you, they will learn to think for themselves and make informed decisions.

Comfort Zones

Communication. You wear your heart and soul on your sleeve, Gemini, and aren't the least bit shy talking about what you feel at any given moment. Scorpio is far more reticent, but during your dating relationship he undoubtedly learned how to open up and to verbalize his feelings. Now that you're married, you should both excel at communication with each other.

Sex. The twins have two distinct approaches to sex. The first twin is the one Scorpio met while you were dating—an audacious flirt who quickly uncovered your common interests and established a personal connection. The second twin is eager to know what makes you tick, who you are in the privacy of your own being, and this twin is the one with whom Scorpio bonds sexually.

Metaphysical Exploration. Your metaphysical explorations, Gemini, fit the five interrogatives you learned in elementary school: who, what, where, when and how? This approach provides structure to Scorpio's quest to uncover the answers to the big questions. What happens when we die? Is there life after death? Is spirit communication possible? Is reincarnation true? You are both comfortable with each other in this area.

Tips
As a mutable air sign, you're the one who is most likely to compromise when you and Scorpio have a disagreement. But if it's something you feel strongly about, don't do it just to keep the peace. Discuss it. Find a way around whatever it is. Here are a few other tips about how to maintain harmony in your marriage to Scorpio:

- ➢ When Scorpio is being dogmatic, call her on it, but gently.
- ➢ Don't rush Scorpio. This can be challenging because you are often so restless and impatient.
- ➢ Nurture your joint creativity.

Unlocking the Secret to Scorpio
Your facility and ease with language and your ability to communicate is the best way to unlock the secret to Scorpio—even if it takes awhile! You'll keep asking questions and communicating how you feel and what you think and eventually, Scorpio will do likewise.

Cancer Married to a Scorpio

The Beauty Within

As discussed in the dating chapter, you and Scorpio are innately private individuals, whose inner worlds are often more real and important to you than the external world. As water signs, you both view life through the lens of your emotions and intuition, and your trust has to be earned. You obviously learned this about each other when you dated and reached the point where you trusted each other enough to get married!

The respective rulers of your signs hold vital clues about how you can fine-tune your compatibility in this marriage. You, Cancer, a cardinal water sign, are ruled by the moon, which represents our capacity to nurture and be nurtured, intuition, emotions and the feminine. The moon represents yin energy. Scorpio's ruler, Pluto, symbolizes profound transformation and regeneration and the co-ruler, Mars, symbolizes physical and sexual energy, individuation, aggression and the warrior in each of us. It's yang.

As water signs, though, you and Scorpio are on the same page with most things. But, as the saying goes, the devil is in the details, so let's take a look at the potential hot spots in this marriage and how they can be mitigated or avoided altogether.

Hot Spots

Joint Finances. Generally, Cancers save their money and aren't lavish spenders, except when it comes to their homes and families. Then, no expense is spared. Scorpio also tends to be a saver, but does spend her money on things that relate to her interests—foreign travel, for instance, or her creative passions. Neither of you should have a problem with the other's expenditures. But if you do—if there's something blatantly unfair about who spends what—then it might be wise to keep your finances separate for the first year or two, and see how things shake out.

With water signs, there can be emotional baggage attached to money and beliefs about money. But by the time you're married, you'll already be aware of that baggage and those beliefs.

Domestic Stuff. Whether you're a man or a woman, Cancer, you're fussy about your domestic environment. For you, there is a place for everything and everything is in its place. This is especially true for the rooms where you spend the most time. The kitchen, for instance, may be the truest reflection of just how orderly you are—foods arranged by type and maybe even alphabetized, fridge so clean and spotless that even the smallest sliver of cheese can be immediately located. Your concept of order, though, may not be Scorpio's idea of order, so this could be a bone of contention.

Your inclination will be to do all the domestic chores. But if you work full-time, this is self-defeating and impractical. You and Scorpio should discuss this early on in your marriage to avoid conflict.

Career. If Scorpio's career takes him away from home frequently and you don't feel secure in the relationship, your imagination may conjure up all the worst possible scenarios. Truth be told, your imagination may cough up those scenarios regardless of what Scorpio does for a living. When you feel like that, take a deep breath and find that grounded center of yourself.

Then throw yourself into your own work, your own career, so you don't have time to ask, *What if?* After all, before you were married, before Scorpio entered your life, your career was probably the focus of your life.

Social Life. Some signs are party animals whose social lives are the center of their universes. Cancer and Scorpio generally don't fall in this category unless they have a lot of fire sign planets in their charts. You and Scorpio tend toward introversion and enjoy your solitude. You don't need to be surrounded by people and acquaintances to feel complete. Your social life as a couple is about quality, not quantity.

Kids. You and Scorpio probably agree on the basics when it comes to your child or children. The area of possible contention lies in your tendency to be overprotective and Scorpio stoking the fires of independence in your kids. If you and Scorpio can strike a balance in this regard, then raising a family will be a joy.

Comfort Zones

You and Scorpio have numerous comfort zones in your marriage, areas that work well because you share a similar emotional and intuitive approach to life. There are some comfort zones, though, that work flawlessly.

Sex. It's within the intimacy of the marriage that you and Scorpio communicate the most profoundly. It's as if you enter the intuitive flow of who you are as individuals and who you are as a couple. It's possible to uncover the lives you have shared in the past, to tap into the strengths and issues brought forward into this life and to discover your souls' purpose in coming together this time around.

Creativity. When you and Scorpio team up on creative projects, you are unsurpassed. Your imaginations and intuitions flow together in such an effortless way that it's as if you are a single brain, a single consciousness. No telling what wonders you might usher into the collective consciousness!

Exploration. Ready to hunt for aliens? Ghosts? Ready to develop your telepathic and precognitive abilities? Any kind of exploration into the unknown, the inexplicable or the mysterious helps to deepen the relationship.

Tips

> ➢ Learn to deal with confrontation. As a cardinal water sign who dislikes confrontation, you will do one of two things when you and Scorpio disagree: you'll give in or remove yourself from the situation. If you give in too often, Scorpio will begin to think you're a pushover. If you walk away too often, Scorpio may think the marriage is no longer important to you. Find a balance.
> ➢ Maintain a healthy sex life. Okay, it sounds like a cliché, but for you and Scorpio, it's one of the bottom lines.
> ➢ Stay positive. Thanks to the moon that rules your sign, your moods shift suddenly and erratically. But you can talk yourself out of a negative space as quickly as you plummet into that space. Be aware, always, of how you feel. Your emotions are the most accurate gauge you have for how your marriage—and your life—are unfolding.

Unlocking the Secret to Scorpio

Your intuition is your most accurate compass in unlocking the secret to your partner. Use it when language is inadequate, when you feel confused or bewildered by something Scorpio says or does. It will enable you to understand what's actually going on inside your spouse.

♌ + ♏
Leo Married to a Scorpio

Dramatic

Your life, Leo, often unfolds like a Shakespearean drama. Since life is your stage, your flamboyance and innate sense of drama find expression in everything you do. You enjoy being the center of attention and surround yourself with admirers. In this regard, you and Scorpio are radically different from each other. It's a difference that can either work beautifully or can spell disaster. Vital clues lie in the planets that govern your respective signs, so let's take a deeper look.

Your sign is ruled by the sun, the very essence and energy of life. This rulership accounts for your boundless optimism, personal magnetism and your need to make an impact in every situation. Scorpio is ruled by transformative Pluto and co-ruled by Mars, the warrior. The combined energies of these two planets account for Scorpio's often serious demeanor and his need to delve deeply into whatever he tackles.

Despite the difference in elements for your respective signs—fire and water—both signs are fixed. It means you are equally relentless in the pursuit of what you want, stubborn and slow to change your beliefs and opinions. In this marriage, both of you must learn the art of compromise.

Hot Spots

Joint Finances. Generally, Leo, when you want something, you buy it. If you can't afford it, you charge it. If your credit cards are maxed out, then you hock the silverware you inherited from your mother. Saving for a rainy day isn't in the picture because for you, there aren't any rainy days! Exceptions exist, of course. If you're a Leo with an earth sign moon—Taurus, Virgo or Capricorn—then you are probably more prone to saving and spending wisely.

You and Scorpio undoubtedly worked out this issue before you tied the knot. But if you didn't, and money is a hot spot in the marriage, sit down immediately and figure out a plan that works for both of you.

Domestic Stuff. Whether you're male or female, domestic stuff interests you only in terms of what you enjoy. If you like to cook, you do so with dramatic touches that spark the palette. If you enjoy grocery shopping, then you make it an adventure. Anything that smacks of a "chore" turns you off. If you and Scorpio can afford it, hire someone to clean your home. If you can't afford it, then come up with a division of labor plan with which you both can live.

Career. You and Scorpio are equally ambitious, with big dreams and goals. You excel at work in front of the public—politics, teaching, acting, theater or anything that has an audience. In business, you're not the middle manager; you're the CEO. Some Scorpios prefer to be the power behind the scenes; others prefer to be recognized as the power figure in the game. It's unlikely that career issues are a hot spot in the marriage. But if they are, it's because you're both so swept up in your professional lives that the marriage doesn't receive the time it deserves.

Social Life. For some Leos, their social lives are a way of expressing their creativity. This type tends to have numerous friends and a vast network of professional and personal acquaintances. For other Leos, their social lives revolve around their families, interests and passions. By the time you and Scorpio are married, you should have a clear sense about each other's preferences in terms of social life. This area won't be a hot spot unless one of you fails to respect the other's boundaries—you throw a party on the night before you or Scorpio has to get up at 5:00 a.m., or you invite friends for an impromptu dinner and forget to tell your partner. Basic consideration goes a long way!

Kids. You, Leo, aren't just a mom or a dad. When it comes to children, you're the head of your tribe. Scorpio gets that and honors it. But be careful that you and Scorpio don't clash over power issues, over who has the final say when it comes to your kids. The final say should be an agreement, and agreements usually involve *compromise.*

Comfort Zones

You and Scorpio have well-defined comfort zones, places where you can retreat together to deepen your relationship. Foremost among these is your respective creative talents.

Creativity. When a Leo and a Scorpio team up as creative partners, the sky really is the limit. Whether you're co-authoring a book or a screenplay, acting or directing, refurbishing your home, raising a family—or all of the above—you complement each other's skills.

Sex. For you and Scorpio, sex and love is a smorgasbord to be savored. You taste, delve and delight in infinite variety. Your directness, Leo, is something that Scorpio appreciates. And you appreciate Scorpio's sensuality, her understanding that you enjoy the game of seduction, the prelude of looks and sexting messages as much as the actual intimacy. You're an ardent, passionate lover, and Scorpio is your match between the sheets, making love to you as though your body is a city of shadows that must be illuminated.

Travel. Most Leos and Scorpios enjoy travel. For Scorpio, there may be a quest or search involved, while for you, it's to see whatever there is to see, to experience new landscapes, people and opportunities. For both of you, travel is creative fodder.

Work. You're both diligent workers who rarely quit what they start. If you can combine business with marriage, no telling what might emerge!

Tips
In order to maintain harmony in your marriage, here are some tips that both you and Scorpio should keep in mind:

> ➢ Avoid possessiveness and jealousy. Both of you are capable of these behaviors and consider them a major turnoff.
> ➢ Scorpio, always applaud and appreciate your partner. Leo, never take Scorpio for granted.
> ➢ Learn to compromise. And take turns compromising. It shouldn't always be the same person who gives in.

Unlocking the Secret to Scorpio
Be yourself. Be who you are stripped of your public persona and your audience. Let down your guard. Once you do this, Scorpio will reveal herself.

♍ + ♏
Virgo Married to a Scorpio

The Journey Within

Ah, well, here we are, you think as you and your Scorpio partner sit across the dinner table from each other. *Now what?* This is the beginning of an inner dialogue that is as familiar to you as your own skin. *What? Why? Where? When? How?* Your mental agility and quickness are like finely tuned instruments, and your attention to detail may be unsurpassed in the zodiac. As a result, you tend to delve as deeply into whatever interests you. In this regard, you and Scorpio are ideally matched. In fact, this combination—with a few minor adjustments—should work well.

You, like Gemini, are ruled by Mercury, the planet that governs communication and travel. Not surprisingly, communication is important to you and some Scorpios aren't particularly communicative—unless it's through telepathy! You and Scorpio probably worked out the communication business while you were dating, but in the event that it's still a diamond in the rough, get busy. You'll have to convince Scorpio about the value of verbalizing what he feels when he feels it and not a week later. And you, in turn, should keep in mind that the two of you don't have to discuss every little detail—even though you would like to!

One possible minefield in this combination? You're extremely self-critical, Virgo, and that critical streak sometimes is turned on other people. Don't criticize Scorpio unless it is really important to draw her attention to something.

Hot Spots

Joint Finances. When you're a big spender, you usually step back at some point and question what you're buying and why. What need does it fill? When you're tight with money, you do the same thing. You follow an arc of evolvement toward perfection in everything you do by analyzing the patterns of your own behavior. Scorpio tends to be a saver, but usually isn't stingy with his money. The two of you should be able to strike a balance in joint finances without it becoming a bone of contention.

Domestic Stuff. A popular image of your sign, Virgo, is that of a person who is compulsively tidy. Some Virgos are, some aren't. If you're the former type of Virgo, then domestic stuff will come natural to you. You'll organize and tidy up without even thinking about it. If you're the latter type of Virgo, you may become resentful if Scorpio expects you to shoulder the bulk of the domestic chores.

Regardless of which type of Virgo you are, it's wise to divide domestic chores based on your various skills and talents. When things feel out of whack, voice it rather than letting things fester.

Career. You're a perfectionist about many things, but particularly about your work. You take great pride in what you do and are diligent in the pursuit of your professional goals and dreams. Scorpio is very much in line with you on this score. This area isn't likely to be a hot spot in the marriage unless you neglect to make time for your partner.

Social Life. Since you and Scorpio enjoy many of the same social activities, this area shouldn't be a hot spot in the marriage unless one of you dislikes the other's friends. If that's the case, then you simply see your respective friends on your own. Don't overthink any of this, Virgo, or allow feelings of insecurity to creep into the picture when Scorpio goes off with her friends.

Kids. Children usually change the dynamics of any marriage. You and Scorpio embrace the experience of being parents, and the only hot spot that may emerge is about the spiritual tradition in which your children are raised. It's likely that you have sampled various spiritual beliefs and have found one that appeals to your practical side. Scorpio has undoubtedly explored different spiritual traditions as well and has found what works for her. If your spiritual beliefs are radically different (unlikely), then your child will have the fortunate opportunity to be exposed to both belief systems.

Comfort Zones

You, as a mutable earth sign, and Scorpio, as a fixed water sign, share several significant comfort zones. Before we explore them, keep in mind that your approach to life generally tends to be more practical than Scorpio's. While Scorpio is searching for the bottom line of whatever she tackles, you're more interested in connecting the dots so that the full picture emerges. Your respective approaches are reflected in all areas of your lives together.

Sex. The misrepresentation of your sexuality, Virgo, is a result of the symbol designated for your sign: the virgin. It leads to the assumption that everyone born under this sign is chaste, a cold fish. Nothing can be further from the truth. You, like Scorpio, are an experimenter, hungry for the deeper connections that intimacy and sex provide. You may not always be aware of this hunger, but it's there in every touch, every caress and every intimate look. It's as if a dormant passion presses against whatever restrictions you have imposed on yourself and screams to be released. And Scorpio is the one to release it.

Creativity. Any kind of creative project you undertake as partners deepens your connection. From a home decoration project to writing a novel or screenplay together, Scorpio will envision the totality of the finished project, and you, Virgo, will connect the dots and lay out the strategy.

Physical Fitness. If you're a Virgo who is health conscious and pays close attention to your diet and general physical fitness—and many Virgos are—then try to find a physical activity that you and your partner enjoy and can do regularly. Make this activity part of your daily routine.

Tips

Post these tips where you'll see the often—your fridge or your bedroom mirror. The list begins with the most important tip for maintaining a harmonious relationship with Scorpio:

- ➤ Keep your criticisms to yourself. Better yet, follow the Dale Carnegie rule of three: Don't criticize, condemn or complain.
- ➤ In a disagreement, it's likely that you'll be the one to give in, to compromise. If you do that often, then Scorpio will assume she'll always get her way!
- ➤ Be honest with each other, always. No exceptions.

Unlocking the Secret to Scorpio

Connect the dots and keep connecting until it all makes sense! No one in the zodiac does this better than you do, Virgo, and every dot, every detail, illuminates some new facet of Scorpio.

Famous Virgo/Scorpio Couples

Kimberly Williams Paisley (Virgo) and Brad Paisley (Scorpio)
Blake Lively (Virgo) and Penn Badgley (Scorpio)

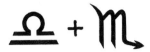

Libra Married to a Scorpio

Romantic

You're the romantic of the zodiac, the one who really does love those moonlit walks on the beach and candlelit dinners in some secluded spot where intimate conversation flourishes. As a cardinal air sign, you can be as passionate as Scorpio, as chatty and charming as Gemini and as rash and impulsive as Aries. But in each instance, your energy is focused on relationships, people, the arts, mediation and a quest for balance and harmony. All of these traits appeal to Scorpio.

Your sign, like Taurus, is ruled by Venus, traditionally the goddess of love, artistic instinct and sociability. Scorpio is ruled by transformative Pluto and co-ruled by aggressive Mars. In other words, Libra, your sign is yin to Scorpio's yang. A balance, right? But the balance can be delicate at times, so let's take a look at the potential hot spots in a marriage between you and Scorpio.

Hot Spots

Joint Finances. Since Venus has some bearing on material resources, earning capacity and spending habits, joint finances can be touchy at times. It's likely that you're a saver, as Scorpio is, but when you have money to burn, you can be a lavish spender, particularly when it comes to the arts, music and your own surroundings. If you and your partner are both employed and earn about the same amount of money, then you might want to consider pooling a certain amount monthly for household expenses and keeping the rest of your finances separate.

Domestic Stuff. Whether you're a man or a woman, you're all about accommodation and cooperation and often bend over backward to avoid confrontation. As a result, you may find yourself doing the bulk of the domestic chores and will grow to resent it. With that in mind, it's best to use your diplomacy and strategic skills to lay out a plan before any of this becomes a real bone of contention in the marriage.

Career. This area probably won't be a hot spot in the marriage. Your respective careers are important to you. And you, Libra, have such an innate sense of fairness that you understand how to balance work and family. And in the event that you forget, Scorpio will remind you!

Social Life. You are so people-oriented, Libra, that your friends are undoubtedly important to you. In the marriage, you're the one who keeps tabs on the social calendar, organizing dinners, parties, family reunions, tickets for concerts and art exhibits. Scorpio is more solitary, and if she decides to bow out of some of the things you plan, that's fine. You've got plenty of friends and acquaintances who would be delighted to join you.

Kids. This area should work well for the marriage. You bring to parenting the same skills you bring to every other area of your life. And Scorpio brings her ability to encourage self-reliance and independence in your kids.

Comfort Zones

Sex. For you, intimacy begins with a look, a touch, a soft laugh or words uttered in a certain way. You're a coy, flirtatious charmer whose facility with language is your most powerful and magnetic means of seduction. Your approach to intimacy fits the aesthetic sensibilities of Venus, and Scorpio is bowled over by it. By the same token, your partner's powerful magnetism awakens you to the full dimension of your own sexuality and in this journey, you learn a great deal about your sexual and emotional needs. See why this part of the marriage is so effortless?

Physical Fitness. Yoga, anyone? This physical activity would be ideal for both of you. It appeals to your aesthetic sensibilities, Libra, and appeals to the deeper part of Scorpio who understands the mind/body connection. The development of flexibility in the body will help you both to develop greater flexibility in the marriage as well.

Creativity. With any joint creative project, you and Scorpio develop a kind of telepathic connection. In this area, you two excel separately and together.

Tips

These tips are a combination of pet peeves and points to remember to keep your marriage harmonious:

> ➤ You really dislike it when Scorpio mistakes you for a pushover. That means, Libra, that in a disagreement, you shouldn't always be the one to give in.
> ➤ When Scorpio tries to control you—and he will—call him on it, as it's happening, not five days later.
> ➤ Be decisive. When you make a decision, stick to it.

Unlocking the Secret to Scorpio

Let your inner psychic play. Keep reading between the lines. Unlocking the secret to your spouse may sometimes feel as impossible as understanding Mona Lisa's smile. But this process of discovery is one at which you excel.

Famous Libra/Scorpio Couples

Katy Perry (Libra) and John Mayer (Scorpio)

Gavin Rossdale (Libra) and Gwen Stefani (Scorpio)

♏ + ♏
Scorpio Married to a Scorpio

An Eternal Mystery

This powerhouse combination blows the socks off lesser mortals. But if you made it through dating and are now married, then you are both obviously comfortable with the emotional and sexual intensity and the transformative nature of this relationship. With this combo, though, a closer look at your respective natal moons can describe the inner dynamics of the marriage.

In astrology, the moon governs our inner worlds, emotions, intuition, the maternal archetype and our capacity to nurture and be nurtured. An earth sign moon—Taurus, Virgo, Capricorn—helps to ground your emotions and colors your intuitive skills with a certain pragmatism. An air sign moon—Gemini, Libra, Aquarius—triggers more verbal communication between the two of you, brings a sociability to the marriage and enables you to view that elusive "bottom line" through the lens of your intellect.

If one or both of you have a fire sign moon—Aries, Leo, Sagittarius—then your willingness to take risks is ramped up and your nomadic restlessness is set in motion. A water sign moon—Cancer, Scorpio, Pisces—enhances your imagination and psychic abilities.

Hot Spots

Joint Finances. Whether this area is a hot spot in the marriage depends on how long you were both single before you got married, your respective incomes and your beliefs about money. If you both tend to be savers, it probably won't be an issue. But if one of you makes less money and spends lavishly, then this area could spell disaster.

Domestic Stuff. Let's face it. Scorpios are about power—how, when and where it's wielded, if it's reined in and why and whether it corrupts or transforms. If you each have certain areas that you rule absolutely and respect those boundaries, then domestic stuff shouldn't be a hot spot. Kingdoms shift with time, however, and it's vital that you exercise flexibility and learn to compromise.

Career. If your respective careers prove to be a hot spot in the marriage, then the relationship may be doomed before you celebrate your first anniversary. That said, if you and your Scorpio partner dated for longer than five minutes, the career area was understood early on. If there were issues, they have been worked out already.

Social Life. In this potential hot spot, there shouldn't be a problem unless one of you has a profusion of planets in a sociable air sign—Gemini, Libra, Aquarius. You and your Scorpio partner usually aren't party animals. Your social activities tend to be with small groups of friends or with like-minded individuals.

Kids. If this area is a hot spot in the marriage, it's probably due to a power struggle about who's in charge. Ideally, you should both be in charge! In terms of the child's spiritual upbringing, you and your partner are probably in agreement.

Comfort Zones

Sex. Elusive, mysterious and sultry are some of the adjectives used to describe your erotic style. But how erotic can sex be in a marriage? Well, for a couple of Scorpios, your sexual intimacy should improve and deepen over the months and years you're together. It is the most reliable gauge about the health of your marriage.

The piercing insights you gain into your partner's psyche are a two-way street when you're married to another Scorpio.

Creativity. Put a couple of Scorpios in a room together to brainstorm and there's no telling what they might create. Your combined intuitive abilities enable you to soar across the universe in search of ideas and what you bring back is scrutinized and analyzed as you dig for the kernel of absolute truth. Like a bit of sand in an oyster's shell, this process eventually renders an exquisite pearl.

Exploration. The exploration could entail anything—an ancient ruin, a foreign country or some facet of the paranormal (ghost hunting, anyone?)—even a new creative venue or talent. However the exploration unfolds, you and your partner relish these excursions.

Tips
Well, this is easy. As a Scorpio married to a Scorpio, you already know what pushes your partner's buttons. The same things that push yours! Here are the big turnoffs:

- ➢ Boastfulness
- ➢ People who are know-it-alls
- ➢ Disloyalty
- ➢ Duplicity
- ➢ Lying
- ➢ Control freaks
- ➢ Manipulative people

There's a certain irony about the last two items on this list. Scorpios can be manipulative and controlling!

Unlocking the Secret to Scorpio
Look within. Allow your piercing insights the freedom to explore all the shadowed corners of your partner's psyche.

Sagittarius Married to a Scorpio

A Quest

Sagittarians seem to come in two broad types. The first type has an unquenchable thirst for experience, which translates into a whirlwind of ideas and action. This type is perpetually primed for adventure. She's the traveler, the truth seeker, the spiritual iconoclast who samples a little of this, a little of that and tries to fit it into a coherent picture of who she is. The second type is trying to understand the bigger picture of life, sees herself as part of the global village and often has one or more humanitarian causes. Which type are you? Are you a meld of both?

Some people will tell you this is a terrible match, that Scorpio is too jealous and possessive and that Sagittarius is too independent and adventurous. They'll tell you that Scorpio is a brooder and that Sagittarius takes nothing seriously. And while all this may be true, it's not the full truth.

There may be times in the marriage when Scorpio is overwhelmed by your relentless energy and you feel like kicking him in the butt so that he'll come out and play with you. Part of the differences between you is due to the respective rulers of your signs. Sagittarius, a mutable fire sign, is ruled by expansive Jupiter, the largest planet in our solar system. In mythology, he was the king of gods. He's the source of your boundless optimism and why you do everything in such a big way. In contrast, Scorpio is ruled by transformative Pluto and co-ruled by Mars, which governs our physicality and sexuality. These two planets are responsible for Scorpio's emotional and sexual intensity.

When you and Scorpio were dating, you probably worked out most of your differences. But dating isn't the same as living with someone 24/7, so let's take a look at the potential hot spots in the marriage.

Hot Spots

Joint Finances. Constraint isn't in your vocabulary. You have so many options when it comes to spending money—travel, education, workshops, seminars, animals, books, movies, more travel… The challenge is that you're married to someone who would rather save than spend.

If you're both working, you should be able to agree upon how much you each contribute toward rent/mortgage, food and other living expenses. It would be wise, Sadge, to take Scorpio's cue and learn how to save a certain amount of what you earn.

Domestic Stuff. If division of household labor is an issue in the marriage, and it may well be, the best solution is to pursue your individual strengths. Who is the best cook? Who is most organized? Who enjoys gardening? If you can't come to an agreement about who does what, and you can afford to hire people to do the domestic stuff, then by all means do so. It will help to maintain harmony in the marriage.

Career. You're happiest in a career where you can call the shots and come and go as you please—small business owner, entrepreneur, actor, writer, Internet marketing agent or, better yet, a professional traveler! Your career is as important to you as Scorpio's career is to her. There shouldn't be any conflict in this area unless one of you works the same hours the other has off.

Social Life. Your versatility and optimism have won you many friends over the years and you continue to nurture and treasure those relationships. So when Scorpio doesn't feel like hitting the road with just a pack and an ATM card, there are plenty of other people to tap for the journey. In other words, your social life doesn't contract just because you're married. As long as Scorpio understands this, it won't be a problem.

Kids. On the surface, it appears that you and Scorpio have vastly different approaches to parenting. But the reality is that your parenting styles may have more in common than either of you realize. You give your children a lot of latitude and believe they should find their own way. You offer broad guidelines and your own wisdom but don't force your opinions. Scorpio strives to create a comfortable, secure home for his children, a refuge from the outside world and encourages their independence by urging them to never accept easy answers.

Comfort Zones

Sex. Your libido doesn't need much stoking, but you do enjoy being cajoled and being made to feel that Scorpio understands you so well that your free-spirited approach to intimacy is appreciated. You're turned on by the here and now, by making love in different places, like outside, under a sky strewn with stars. Scorpio has no problem accommodating your preferences.

Physical Fitness. Your preference for physical fitness may be team sports or group activities and Scorpio's preference may be for more solitary pursuits. However, you definitely agree on the importance of staying fit. The kinds of food you like or dislike probably won't be so vastly different that one of you is a vegetarian and the other is a meat eater. But if that's the case, is it really a big deal?

Creativity. You enjoy thinking outside the box and you don't hesitate taking risks creatively, particularly if those risks might benefit the larger family of man. Your brainstorming for ideas usually starts with *what if,* and Scorpio's often begins with an exploration of metaphor. While you're seeking the bigger picture, Scorpio is seeking the bottom line. This combination is sure to produce a winner!

Tips

> ➤ If Scorpio becomes possessive—and he may—don't get angry and argue about it. Simply call him on it. It's the best way to avert disaster.
>
> ➤ If you feel your freedom is being restricted in some way, don't lash out with sarcasm. Disengage, call a friend and get out and about.
>
> ➤ Neither of you should tell the other how to live their life.
>
> ➤ At the first sign of emotional manipulation—from you or Scorpio—back off.

Unlocking the Secret to Scorpio

Keep looking for the larger picture, how the marriage fits into the bigger scheme of things for you both. It's a quest, right, Sadge?

Famous Sagittarius/Scorpio Couples

Tina Turner (Sagittarius) and Ike Turner (Scorpio)—an example of when things really go wrong with this combination

Phil Donahue (Sagittarius) and Marlo Thomas (Scorpio)

Steven Spielberg (Sagittarius) and Kate Capshaw (Scorpio)—an example of when this combination really works well

Capricorn Married to a Scorpio

Conquering Duo

So here you are, Capricorn, married and loving it. Now you and your partner can build together—a family, career, business or reputation, something that endures. Both of you are capable of tremendous focus and determination, and once you set your sights on something, you pursue it. Your methods vary, but complement each other. When you encounter an obstacle, you find a way around it. When Scorpio encounters an obstacle, he digs until he finds out why the obstacle exists, where its weakness is and then obliterates it.

Your cardinal earth sign is ruled by Saturn, the planet that represents discipline, hard work and the building of foundations. It teaches us what we need to learn in order to grow and evolve. Scorpio, a fixed water sign, is ruled by transformative Pluto, the planet that symbolizes power, profound transformation and regeneration. It's co-ruled by Mars, which symbolizes our physical energy, individualism, action and sex drive.

There probably won't be many hot spots in this marriage, but disagreements may surface that involve power. Who's in charge? Who's the boss? Both you and Scorpio can be control freaks, so this issue will have to be ironed out. Let's take a look at specific areas that hold potential problems.

Hot Spots

Joint Finances. The image of the goat that represents your sign, Capricorn, symbolizes your slow, steady rise in the world, the way you build your career one step at a time. You build your finances in the same way, one penny at a time. Like Scorpio, you're thrifty, but you do go through periods when you overspend. These spending sprees usually involve the acquisition of material goods that reflect what you seek or involve less tangible things like travel, dance lessons. As long as you're contributing a fair share to your joint living expenses, this area shouldn't be a problem.

Domestic Stuff. Because your sign and Scorpio are naturally compatible, the division of domestic chores should be easy. You each do whatever you're good at. If this area becomes a hot spot now and then, it will probably be due to your respective busy schedules rather than to laziness or disinterest.

Career. You're both industrious, relentless workers, personally and professionally. This area shouldn't be a hot spot unless your careers entail a lot of travel and time away from home and each other.

Social Life. Your social lives aren't about rock and roll and partying on forever. When you do get together with friends, there's often a purpose larger than enjoyment—networking, for instance, or the exploration of a new place, concept or creative project. Your social lives and business lives often overlap.

Kids. Whether you're male or female, Capricorn, you're a devoted parent and bring an almost businesslike efficiency to the job. Due to the influence of Saturn that rules your sign, you can be a bit too rigid with your kids at times and Scorpio can be overprotective. Yet, you both encourage independent thinking in your children and value education.

Comfort Zones

Generally, this combination is so compatible that your comfort zones are numerous, and any disagreement, even in the potential hot spot areas, is resolved fairly easily. Part of this is attributable to your ability to stand up to Scorpio when you need to.

Sex. You and Scorpio probably tie as the most sexual signs in the zodiac. People expect it of Scorpio, but not of you. Scorpio's sexuality is more public, more obvious and apparent in her smoldering eyes and the way she carries herself. Your lusty libido is rarely on public display. In the intimacy of your own bedroom, though, your carnality roars out of hiding and your libido doesn't need much coaxing. Your and Scorpio's challenge is to not spend your entire marriage in bed!

Physical Fitness. As an earth sign, physical exercise is probably part of your daily routine and if it isn't, it should be! You and Scorpio should find something physical (other than sex) that you enjoy doing together. It doesn't matter what it is—the gym, Pilates, hiking, rock climbing, jogging or brisk walks—as long as you both like it and can integrate it into your daily routines.

Creativity. You're methodical and consistent in your creativity and are an expert at finding what you need when you need it. Scorpio's approach to creativity is intuitive, intense and can often be spiritual, too. When you two combine talents on any creative project—whether it's redecorating your home or writing the great American novel—Scorpio envisions, and you implement.

Tips

You and Scorpio are turned off by many of the same behaviors and attributes—dishonesty, hypocrisy, gossips, duplicity, quitters, manipulators and disloyalty. So this bulleted list of tips is primarily a reminder about your own behaviors toward each other that can help to maintain harmony in your marriage.

> ➤ If you get into a power struggle, evaluate what the issue actually concerns. Is it worth a standoff? If so, hold your ground. If not, let it go.
> ➤ Since you're both workaholics, be sure to carve out time daily for each other. It's much too easy for you to be swept up in the thrill of your professional lives.
> ➤ If you are annoyed by something your partner is doing, voice it, as it's happening, not a month later!

Unlocking the Secret to Scorpio

Do it a step at a time, methodically, with heart and soul.

Famous Capricorn/Scorpio Couples

Jim Carrey (Capricorn) and Jenny McCarthy (Scorpio)

Jason Segel (Capricorn) and Chloë Sevigny (Scorpio)

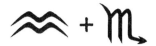

Aquarius Married to a Scorpio

Paradigm Busters

Just to be clear from the get-go, there's no such thing as a typical Aquarian. You already knew that, of course, but are nonetheless delighted to hear it. You're a true nonconformist, as much a rebel as Sagittarius and often as inscrutable as Scorpio. You're a visionary who sees opportunity where others may see only obstacles and hardship. Other people—even your Scorpio partner—may see you as a bundle of contradictions. But the bottom line is fairly simple: no one can tell you what to do or how to do it, and you refuse to accept something as true just because someone tells you so. In this regard, you and Scorpio, both fixed signs, are on the same page.

This combination may not be one of the easiest, but it's certainly one of the most intriguing. The main impediment to harmony is that you, Aquarius, are a communicator who can talk about what you think or feel—or both—at any time. Scorpio is more reticent. The planets that rule your respective signs hold significant clues about how this marriage works.

Aquarius, a fixed air sign, is ruled by Uranus, the planet that governs abrupt, unforeseen change, your individuality, genius, eccentricity, breaks with tradition and old patterns. Scorpio is ruled by transformative Pluto and co-ruled by Mars, which governs our physical energy and sexuality. You each have something to bring to the proverbial table, and you both prize your freedom and independence. But because you're both fixed signs, compromise may be difficult to achieve. Let's take a look at the potential hot spots and how they can be mitigated.

Hot Spots

Joint Finances. For you, the accumulation of wealth isn't the point. Money simply spells freedom. You're generous with your family and loved ones and also give to causes you believe in and to friends in need. Scorpio is fine with all this. The one possible glitch in this area could occur if Scorpio insists on investing your money for you. Before you categorically say no, keep in mind that Scorpio is an artist when it comes to investments.

Domestic Stuff. Even though you live a lot of your life in your own head, you tend to be an organized individual for whom everything has its place. The domestic chore area works best when you and Scorpio clean up after yourselves and share the rest according to your respective skills.

Career. What is most important for you in terms of your work and career is freedom. If you have that, then it's likely other areas of your life are humming along well. If you're fortunate enough to be working in a field you enjoy, then this area won't be a hot spot in the marriage.

Social Life. You're a natural networker who enjoys hanging out with friends, meeting eccentric and artistic people, canvassing for your favorite political candidates and generally being in the thick of things about which you feel passionate. Scorpio is more of a loner. This area may not have been an issue when you were dating, but now that you're married, it could become a hot spot. It's best to discuss it—if Scorpio will. Instead, he may brood and go all silent on you.

Kids. Despite your differences, you and Scorpio should agree on most points when it comes to parenting. You both encourage independence and self-reliance in your children, but Scorpio's overprotectiveness may irritate you at times and that could stir up trouble. Neither of you are very good at compromise, and all too often your disagreements end in stalemates. Perhaps it's time to change that!

Comfort Zones

With you and Scorpio, comfort zones must be created, nurtured and molded from your respective needs and expectations. So let's look at the possibilities.

Sex. As with your air sign cousin, Gemini, seduction for you must begin in the mind. Forget the moonlit walks on a deserted beach, the poetry and the music. You crave being teased by ideas, when you share thoughts, dreams and expectations. By now, Scorpio understands this about you; so, don't be surprised when she brings out a book about the Druids and Stonehenge and two round trip tickets to England.

Creativity. With your innate visionary talents and ability to spot future cutting edge trends and Scorpio's powerful intuition, you excel at creative brainstorming. Once you find an idea that excites you both, you dive into it with passion.

Professional Ambitions. When the two of you team up as business partners, your approach is totally unconventional and radically different. You bust paradigms professionally.

Tips

Some astrologers say this combination simply won't work for the long term. There is too much jealousy and emotional manipulation from Scorpio and excessive detachment from you, Aquarius. But the truth is that any combination can work if the individuals involved want it to work. *We* write the script of our lives; astrology is a tool, a beacon, not a master! With that in mind, here are some tips to maintain harmony in your marriage:

➢ When Scorpio broods, don't ask why. Just ignore it and do your own thing.

➢ If Scorpio feels left out because you are so caught up in your own head, she should bring you back to the here and now with a caress, a touch or a kiss.

➢ Patience reaps rewards.

Unlocking the Secret to Scorpio

Use your unconventional intellect and visionary ability to unlock the secret to Scorpio.

Famous Aquarius/Scorpio Couples

Ashton Kutcher (Aquarius) and Demi Moore (Scorpio)

Abhishek Bachchan (Aquarius) and Aishwaryra Rai Bachchan (Scorpio)

Pisces Married to a Scorpio

Imagine!

The fish and the scorpion: does it sound like an oxymoron? What could you and Scorpio possibly have in common? Quite a bit, actually, as you discovered while you were dating. In fact, Pisces and Scorpio are one of the best love matches.

As water signs, you both view the world through your emotions, intuition and by engaging your imaginations. You, however, are so attuned to the emotional environment of people around you that you often absorb their emotions like a psychic sponge. As a result, it's important for you to have time alone so you can detach and center yourself. Scorpio is such an emotionally intense person that you may have to do this rather frequently until you learn to adjust your receptivity. Otherwise, you and Scorpio are deeply compatible. The rulers of your respective signs provide significant clues about your differences.

Your sign is ruled by elusive Neptune, which provides you with a profound connection to the unconscious—your own and that of the collective. Pisces is co-ruled by expansive Jupiter, the planet of luck, serendipity and expansion. The combination of ruling planets endows you with untethered optimism and a psychic ability that is equal to Scorpio's. Your partner's sign is ruled by transformative Pluto and co-ruled by Mars, which governs our sexuality, physical energy and individualism. This combo is why Scorpio may sometimes seem to be obsessed with the esoteric, the unknown and the strange!

Let's take a look at the potential hot spots in a marriage and see how you and Scorpio measure up.

Hot Spots

Joint Finances. Generally, you're less concerned about money and material goods than you are about enjoying what you do to make a living. You don't have any problem in joining financial resources and are even okay with Scorpio investing your money for you. This area isn't likely to be a hot spot in the marriage. But if it is, it might be due to Scorpio trying to control your joint finances without letting you in on the details.

Domestic Stuff. Whether you're a man or a woman, your home reflects your creative expression. You refuse to be limited or restricted by anyone who might inhibit your freedom to express yourself. If Scorpio attempts to do this, the marriage will probably be over rather quickly. Even though you compromise in other areas, you won't compromise about this. You'll do your fair share of domestic stuff as long as Scorpio doesn't cross this line.

Career. Arts, drama, music and invention: you can excel in any area where your creative expression shines. You could also do well as a practicing psychic. It's unlikely that Scorpio will ever knowingly interfere with your career or make demands about it. The same is true for you and Scorpio's career. Again, this is an area that shouldn't be a problem in the marriage. You applaud each other's talents and accomplishments.

Social Life. If hot spots develop in this area, it could be due to your ambivalence and indecisiveness. The image for your sign is of two fish swimming in opposite directions, symbolic of the perennial battle between your head and your heart, each one whispering, *Follow me, follow me....* While this indecisiveness usually pertains to your love life, it can also involve friends or even something as simple as, *Should we go to a movie or take in an art exhibit?* When in doubt, toss a coin. Or ask your question and open a dictionary at random and point at a word on the page. More often than not, the word will give you your answer.

Kids. The potential trouble with this area could center on power—who's in charge? Which parent calls the shots? As a parent, you share a deep psychic connection with your children and often know what they're feeling even if they don't understand it themselves. Scorpio can be overprotective with his children and, at times, too controlling. Yet, you both encourage independent thinking in your kids and nurture their creative gifts.

Comfort Zones

Sex. For you, sex and intimacy are a magical mystery tour, a journey into realms so varied they are physical, emotional, spiritual and may become a point of transcendence. Your sexual electricity and magnetism delights Scorpio and with you, intimacy for Scorpio reaches new heights.

Exploration. You're both intrigued by the paranormal, the mysterious and the unknown and are equipped with the intuition and raw psychic ability to delve into these areas. These explorations can take you virtually anywhere on the planet for a quest, to explore a ruin or to swim with dolphins. Your explorations will usually have a spiritual component.

Creativity. Bring it on! When you and Scorpio combine your imaginations, intuition and talents, the sky is literally the limit for what you may produce.

Tips

As a mutable water sign, you're the one most likely to compromise in a disagreement. So be forewarned: learn to stand up for yourself and your beliefs. Otherwise, Scorpio will come to believe you're a pushover. Always use your considerable imagination to understand what may elude your conscious, rational mind when it comes to figuring out this relationship.

Unlocking the Secret to Scorpio

Unleash your psychic ability and dive into Scorpio's psyche.

Famous Pisces/Scorpio Couples

Kurt Russell (Pisces) and Goldie Hawn (Scorpio)
Liz Taylor (Pisces) and Richard Burton (Scorpio)

Chapter 4:

Scorpio Mom, Scorpio Dad

"Scorpio will not pay a false compliment to gain a point or to win an ally."
- Astrologer Linda Goodman

If one (or both) of your parents is a Scorpio, then you may already be aware of some of what you'll read in this chapter. But other parts of it may be entirely new to you. If you're still in your teens and have picked up this book, then it's likely you have some questions about mom or dad. By the same token, if you're an adult, your Scorpio parent may still be an enigma to you, mysterious and unknowable.

If your mom is a Scorpio, then it's likely you understood early on that she isn't like other mothers. When you were younger, she kept pretty close tabs on you and this was true whether she was a stay-at-home mom or worked full-time. Because of her exacting standards, you can be sure that if you were in childcare, then the facility was one she had researched and visited before you even stepped foot in the place. She might have even run background checks on the employees!

In your teens, these same exacting standards held. If you were going over to a friend's house, she wanted to know if the parents would be home, who else would be there and, yes, she expected you home for dinner. Yet, when it came time to get your driver's license, she was all for it. Driving is a huge step toward independence, and she was eager for you to fly on your own.

At every stage of your relationship, you sensed your mother's passion, intensity and support for you and your endeavors. But you may also have felt there were pockets within her you would never know, secret worlds she didn't invite you to share. And yet, her bond with you runs deep. Whether you live on the other side of the country or in the next town, she often seems to know what you're thinking and feeling, when you're in trouble and when you're jubilant.

Your Scorpio dad is intense, passionate and private, all the adjectives we've come to expect from Scorpio. He may be overprotective at times but is determined to make sure you and the rest of the family are provided for to the best of his ability.

If he's working at what he enjoys, that passion becomes one of the cornerstones of your life. You learn the importance of working in a career that allows you to evolve creatively, spiritually and emotionally on every level. From him you also learn the value of hard work, persistence and listening to your hunches and gut feelings.

If you're in your teens, then your dad has set up clear parameters about what he expects from you and is likely to be strict about some things—how you spend your time and with whom, your diligence about school work and helping out at home. If you're an adult, he's your cheerleader, always in your court, applauding your accomplishments and urging you to do your best.

Your dad, like his female counterpart, may have difficulty expressing his emotions. He may not be the kind of guy who, as he drops you off at school, hugs you good-bye and says, *Love you.* But he's undoubtedly the emotional center of your family, the one who understands what you feel even when you may not understand it yourself. He's something of an oxymoron, a mystery and a puzzle to you, and no matter how you move the pieces around, you'll never figure him out.

Aries Child & Scorpio Parent

Dynamic
Your pioneering spirit may make your Scorpio parent gray before his time. Even so, he admires your independence, fearlessness, leadership abilities and the way you stand up for yourself. Astrologically, this relationship isn't the easiest to navigate, so let's take a look at how you, Aries, can best deal with a Scorpio parent.

Getting Along
Mars, the Roman god of war, rules your sign and co-rules Scorpio. This shared rulership means your Scorpio parent understands your physicality, your need to be in charge and your blunt honesty. And you understand your parent's need to control everything. Avoid butting heads over power issues, and join your parent in some sort of physical activity or sport. This is where you two will shine together.

You're terrific at initiating things, but when you lose interest in whatever it is, you walk away and don't finish it. This will drive your Scorpio parent nuts. Practice patience and persistence. Your Scorpio parent has plenty of both. The guidelines below are for an Aries child of any age.

Simple Guidelines
In order to maintain a harmonious relationship with a Scorpio parent, post this bulleted list where you'll see it often!

> ➤ Don't lie. You're usually bluntly honest when you're asked something, and even if it's not what your Scorpio parent wants to hear, the truth is preferable.

- ➢ Avoid power struggles.
- ➢ Avoid emotional outbursts. If you're angry, take a couple of deep breaths, bite your tongue and walk away until you've calmed down.
- ➢ Never stifle your need to know. At every stage of your life, your inquisitiveness propels you to become a pioneer and to explore what others don't. Your Scorpio parent enjoys answering your questions, so ask away!

Family Vacations/Reunions with a Scorpio

You, like your fire sign cousin Sagittarius, are happiest when a vacation happens spontaneously, when you're flying by the seat of your pants, primed for whatever adventures the universe throws your way. A family vacation with a Scorpio parent, however, is probably going to be more scheduled and rigid than you like. It could be something along the lines of: *Monday, the Grand Canyon, Tuesday, the Four Corners, Wednesday, the Hopi reservation....* And this is where you should pipe up and suggest time to really explore each of the areas. Don't whine and carry on about it, but back it up with facts about why the exploration is needed. After all, you're a member of the family, and it's your vacation, too!

How to Get Your Way

Getting your way with a Scorpio parent is challenging. As a cardinal fire sign, you want everything yesterday, and that just isn't going to happen with your mom or dad. Diplomacy, patience and facts will get you what you want faster than rebellion, emotional outbursts and pulling an attitude.

The Bigger Picture

In the cosmic scheme of things, astrology represents *potential*—not fate. You chose your parents and the circumstances into which you were born so that you could achieve that potential and evolve spiritually, creatively and emotionally at every level.

Your Scorpio parent will never shy away from answering your questions, particularly questions about inner realms—dreams, past lives and spiritual belief systems. He knows that the inspiration and creativity of your sign is best served by open discussion and honesty in all things.

Even if your parent is sometimes reticent, he can't resist answering your questions. This has been true since you were a youngster and plied him with questions about some of the biggies: *What is God? What are angels? What are spirits? Do trees have spirits? Do animals have souls?*

The Challenge

Central to this relationship is your ability to understand why your Scorpio parent behaves as she does. This holds true regardless of your age. If your childhood was difficult because of your Scorpio parent and the issues have carried forward into your adult life, then it's time to figure out why the relationship has been challenging. What are you supposed to learn from this parent? Is there a past-life theme that has carried over into this life? If possible, talk to your parent about your feelings. Sometimes, that's all it takes to resolve a long-standing issue.

Taurus Child & Scorpio Parent

Stable

You and your Scorpio parent should get along well at most stages in your life. As opposite signs, you strike a strong balance—you have strengths that Scorpio doesn't and vice versa. You, as a fixed earth sign ruled by Venus, and Scorpio, a fixed water signed ruled by Pluto and co-ruled by Mars, are equally stubborn, and this is where things could get rough.

Getting Along

Both you and your Scorpio parent enjoy sports and physical activities. Your mom or dad understands your need to be outdoors, hiking, running and competing in sports. When you're still in school and living at home, your parent helps you make room in your schedule for these activities.

You tend to be as secretive as your Scorpio parent. This could be a problem when you're in your teens, and all that hormonal rebellion is bubbling around inside you. But your rebellion isn't like that of other signs. You might sneak out of the house in the middle of the night to feed a stray dog. Or you and a friend might grab your sleeping bags and head out into an open field to sleep under the stars. If you try drugs, it won't be a total immersion in a drug culture. It will be to experiment, to sample; it's part of your individuation process.

Trust your intuition about how much to reveal to your Scorpio parent. You fit the adage that still waters run deep, Taurus, and for your own peace of mind, it's best to avoid confrontations with your Scorpio parent. Be stubborn about what's important to you. Otherwise, try to be flexible.

Simple Guidelines

As a Venus ruled sign, you're a gentle, compassionate person who enjoys being surrounded by beauty and by nature. But you do have buttons that set you off, and when they're pushed once too often, you blow up—*the bull's rush*. Rather than blowing up at your Scorpio parent when she pushes one of those buttons, retreat to some spot you've created for yourself and cool off. It's one of the best ways to maintain harmony in your relationship. Here are some other tips:

➢ You and Scorpio are both infinitely patient. If you think you can outwait a Scorpio until he changes his mind so you can get what you want, you may be waiting an eternity. The reverse may also be true. It's best for both of you to decide if what you want is really worth your time and patience. This is how you both learn the art of compromise.

> It's unlikely that you or Scorpio will lie about anything. But sometimes, blunt honesty that may hurt the other person isn't the way to go, either. If you both soften your approach, no one gets hurt.

> Since Scorpio has difficulty expressing emotions, it's up to you to do so—verbally and non-verbally. A hug and an *I love you*.

Family Vacations/Reunions with a Scorpio

When you were a kid, a family vacation anywhere was always an adventure for you. It was a chance to explore and to taste, see and experience other places. Yes, the schedule might have been a bit rigid at times, but at least you were somewhere new.

As you've gotten older, though, you may be restless to get away from the family and out on your own to explore. If you're a teenager still in school, your Scorpio parent is likely to challenge you on this. After all, if you live on your own, Scorpio can't control the situation—or you! But remain firm in your conviction, particularly if you've got a job and are earning money of your own.

How to Get Your Way

Remember the book *The Little Engine That Could?* In the story, a long train has to be pulled over a high mountain, and all the large engines refuse to try. When a little engine is asked to try, it accepts the challenge. It's a struggle for such a small engine to pull such a long train up such a high mountain. But it keeps repeating, *I think I can, I think I can…*and succeeds. Persistence and belief: that's how you get your own way with Scorpio.

The Bigger Picture

In the cosmic scheme of things, astrology represents *potential*—not fate. You chose your parents and the circumstances into which you were born so that you could achieve that potential and evolve spiritually, creatively and emotionally, at every level. When you're feeling somewhat put out by your Scorpio parent, ask yourself what you're supposed to learn from him. And what is he supposed to learn from you? What are the spiritual underpinnings of this relationship?

If you can't find the answer to those questions, then head out into nature, where you sense the spiritual most intimately and sense the way all of life is connected.

The Challenge

You and your Scorpio parent are equally stubborn. He believes he's right, that his way is the only way. Maybe he's correct, but that's something you have to discover on your own. The trick is doing it so that Scorpio doesn't think you're dismissing his advice just to be contrary. Diplomacy with this parent may be difficult, but it's necessary in order for this relationship to function smoothly.

Gemini Child & Scorpio Parent

Wild & Unpredictable

Here's the thing your Scorpio parent noted early on about you. You aren't just one person; you're two, the twins. One twin is possessed of endless energy and flits around like some magnificent butterfly, sampling a little of this, a little of that. This twin is funny, chatty and has a zillion friends. The other twin is moodier, more circumspect and bookish. On any given day, your Scorpio parent isn't sure which twin is in attendance. And this is true regardless of your age. For both of you, this can present dilemmas.

Mercury, the ruler of your sign, governs communication, so you're usually spontaneous, ready to talk about anything and everything. You, as the saying goes, wear your heart on your sleeve. Your Scorpio parent, however, is reticent and doesn't express emotions easily. When you were a kid, this may have prompted you to wonder if she loved you. As an adult, you understand that people express love in different ways. Chances are that over the years of your maturation, your Scorpio parent learned to be more emotionally expressive.

The primary difference between the two of you is that the lens through which you perceive yourself and the world is intellectual, through the mind and ideas. Scorpio's lens is emotions and intuition. It may not sound like such a big deal, but it can be.

Getting Along

Thanks to your innate curiosity about everything, you have a constant barrage of questions—for yourself or for anyone who will listen. Your Scorpio parent is not only a good listener, but has a wealth of knowledge he's eager to share when the right questions are asked. So ask away, Gemini. Question everything. This question and answer process will help pave a smoother relationship between you and your parent. It will also help Scorpio loosen up in terms of his emotional expression.

Simple Guidelines

As a mutable sign who can be something of a chameleon, you may be the one who has to back down or compromise in a disagreement with your Scorpio parent. You may have to be the one who shrugs like it's no big deal and says, *Yeah, okay, whatever,* when what you really feel like doing is telling him off.

If it concerns something that's really important to you, then have your facts researched and be ready to offer them as a bullet list. You can talk circles around almost anyone, but with a Scorpio parent, facts make the difference and may swing the tide in your favor. Here are some other tips for keeping your relationship with a Scorpio parent more harmonious:

> ➢ Don't rush your Scorpio parent. If you're in a hurry—and you usually are—just head out on your own to do whatever you're going to do. Eventually, Scorpio will get the hint.
> ➢ If your parent sets limits that you don't agree with it, ask why. Ask for an explanation. It may be that Scorpio is simply in his overprotective mode and your asking for an explanation will snap him out of it.
> ➢ Don't always be the one to give in. Scorpio must learn the art of compromise, particularly with a Gemini child.

Family Vacations/Reunions with a Scorpio

Thanks to your innate curiosity, you're happy to travel anywhere, under any circumstances. You're so flexible that even a rigid itinerary set up by Scorpio is fine with you—up to a point. And that point is reached when you're an adult. The ideal family vacation as adults is picking several must-see spots and leaving the rest open to chance and synchronicity!

If you're at a family reunion at your parents' home, then you may have to go with the flow that Scorpio has set up. Just relax and enjoy it.

How to Get Your Way

When you are between the ages of fourteen to twenty-one, your Scorpio parent needs the patience of a saint to deal with you. It's the time when you are pushing hardest against limitations and restrictions that may be imposed on you. To get your way during this time, it's smart to sit down and discuss your concerns with your Scorpio parent. Don't get angry or emotional; just engage Scorpio in conversation.

Once you pass the age of twenty-one, Scorpio won't try to restrict you, unless he's paying your college bills. Then he may try to use money as a means of control. He isn't doing it to be mean. It's just his last hold over you, his final attempt to protect you.

The Bigger Picture

Many Scorpios come into life with an awareness of other dimensions and of the soul's purpose for this life. If your parent is one such Scorpio, then you probably discovered early on that your mom or dad has specific, fixed ideas about the cosmic biggies—life after death, reincarnation and spirituality. As a Gemini, you're more of a sampler when it comes to spirituality. You research, explore, read and may try this belief or that one until you come up with a belief system that fits you.

Where things for a Scorpio are usually black-and-white, true or not true, few things are that starkly contrasted for you. You can live a long time with contradictions in your core beliefs, but at some point, the contradictions catch up with you. If you're an animal lover, for example, you may eventually find that you can no longer eat meat and become a vegetarian. Such drastic reversals in your beliefs reflect your greatest strength—your intellect. For your Scorpio parent, that strength lies in his emotions and piercing intuition.

The Challenge

Yes, you're the communicator of the family and you have a marvelous facility with language. But it's important for you to understand that verbalizing every feeling may not be second nature to your Scorpio parent. So if there are issues in your relationship, Gemini, spell it out in an email or letter. This kind of communication gives her time to think about what you've written and to respond when she's ready.

Cancer Child & Scorpio Parent

Intuitive

You're as emotional and sensitive as your Scorpio parent. The differences between you, though, are as obvious as the symbols that represent your respective signs: a crab and a scorpion. When you're confronted with an issue you don't want to deal with, you crawl into your shell and move like the crab—sideways—to avoid a head-on confrontation. When Scorpio is in the same situation, she either reacts with stinging sarcasm or turns within to dig for answers.

And yet, because you're both water signs, your emotions and intuition are the lens through which you see the world. For you, Cancer, your emotions are your intuitive connection to life. Many Cancers are homebodies. If you're one of them, then your home is important to you, and your Scorpio parent will make sure you always feel secure and protected at home. In fact, Scorpio probably does this better than most signs. Generally, you and your Scorpio parent share such a strong psychic connection that the relationship is relatively smooth.

Getting Along

Your sign is ruled by the moon, which symbolizes your inner world, emotions, intuition, the feminine and the mother. Its energy is yin. By contrast, the energy of Scorpio's co-ruler Mars is yang. And this is where conflict may surface. At times, Scorpio's intensity and passion may overwhelm you to the point where you feel smothered. Rather than withdrawing into your shell, which only bewilders Scorpio, physically remove yourself from the situation. Take your dog to the park, go hiking or hit the gym.

Once you do this enough times, Scorpio learns to back off and give you some space.

Simple Guidelines

Consider this list to be just a reminder of how to maintain a truly harmonious relationship with your Scorpio parent:

> ➤ Encourage conversation. Yes, you and your mom or dad have a telepathic connection, but even telepathy is no substitute for real conversation. Express what you're feeling, make that your standard. Eventually, Scorpio will do so as well.
> ➤ Embark on psychic explorations with Scorpio. Join him in his research, his eternal quest for the absolute bottom line. Your intuitive skills are just as penetrating as Scorpio's and when you team up, there's no telling what mysteries of the universe you might uncover.
> ➤ Always express your love and appreciation for Scorpio—verbally and in ways both large and small.

Family Vacations/Reunions with a Scorpio

You are probably happiest on a vacation when you can take your home along with you—a camper would be ideal. But you would settle for a tent and a campfire, too. If Scorpio isn't keen on either of those options, then the next best thing would be a cabin rental at your destination. That way, you've got a home away from home and can explore the area with the cabin as your base.

Scorpio may try to control every step of the vacation and if you're in your teens or twenties, this kind of control won't be acceptable to you. So— very gently—suggest alternatives. *Let's do such and such instead of….* In this way, Scorpio learns to loosen up his tight control over every situation.

How to Get Your Way

When there's something you really want, the best way to get it is by using your intuition. Find a spot where you won't be interrupted for five or ten minutes and sit down. Shut your eyes, deepen your breathing, and as you begin to relax, pose a question to yourself. *What's the best way to approach Mom (or Dad) about _____ (fill in the blank)?*

Then focus just on the sound and rhythm of your breathing. An image, the refrain from a song, a phrase, the title of a book or perhaps, just a single word will drift into your awareness. If it's not immediately obvious what it means, let it sit for a while. The answer will come to you. Then approach Scorpio and see what happens.

The Bigger Picture

Your family is your tribe. From the time you're old enough to understand this, it's through them that you feel spiritual connections most strongly. As you mature, your tribe expands to friends, your immediate community, the society in which you live and perhaps, even your country. It's through this tribal association that you express your spirituality and beliefs.

Scorpio's journey is more solitary but just as rich in scope. There will always be common ground for the two of you and your spiritual/metaphysical beliefs.

The Challenge

If you feel that your Scorpio parent made your childhood difficult and have carried those feelings forward into your adult life, then these unresolved issues may be holding you back in some way. Use your intuition to drill through these feelings, to understand them and then release them. The release part of this process may be the real challenge.

♌ + ♏
Leo Child & Scorpio Parent

Creative

For you, the approval of others and your self-expression are often paramount to your happiness. You undoubtedly got enough approval from your Scorpio parent as a youngster and probably still do today, regardless of your age. And Scorpio always urges you to express yourself creatively. But because you are both fixed sides of different elements, there may be a number of times when you face off with your Scorpio parent and both of you learn the true meaning of stubbornness—and of compromise.

Getting Along

Your sign is ruled by the sun, the very essence of life; and Scorpio is ruled by transformative Pluto, which plumbs the depths of everything it touches, and co-ruled by Mars, the warrior. You are up front about what you feel and usually express it when you feel it, and Scorpio is far more reticent about what she feels. One way or another throughout your lives as child and parent, this issue surfaces repeatedly until it's resolved.

If you have a water sign moon—Cancer, Scorpio, Pisces—or your parent has a fire sign moon—Aries, Leo, Sagittarius—then this may not be much of an issue at all.

Simple Guidelines

As a Leo adult, you may still have the same questions you did as a kid about getting along with your Scorpio parent. Here are some guidelines for creating a more harmonious relationship. Post them where you'll see them often!

- Choose your battles carefully. When you and Scorpio disagree on something that's important to you, stand your ground. Otherwise, find a way to compromise. The same goes for your Scorpio parent.
- Your flair for the dramatic can get tedious, particularly when it's something you use to get what you want. So before you make your case in any dispute, shake off the drama and gather your facts; then present your evidence with the collected cool of an attorney.
- Diplomacy and creative solutions take you and Scorpio much further than rigid demands and expectations.

Family Vacations/Reunions with a Scorpio

If your parent is one of those Scorpios who plans the family vacation down to the last detail, you probably don't have any problem with it. When you were younger, though, you probably wanted to bring a friend along—or several!—or insisted on having some say in your destinations.

As an adult, perhaps a married adult with a family of your own, family vacations and reunions could be troublesome simply because you're the king or queen in your own home and don't like being told what to do or how you're doing something wrong. Just remember that the vacation won't last forever, so bite your tongue, Leo, and go along with the flow.

How to Get Your Way

No drama. No theatrics. First, visualize Scorpio giving in or compromising with you. Back the visualization with emotion. *Feel* it. Imagine what it would be like to get your way about this particular thing you so desire. Pretend you are already living it. *Act as though you're living it.* Then gather your facts about why you should get your way, present them to Scorpio calmly and say nothing more about it. But keep visualizing and acting as though you've already gotten your way.

The Bigger Picture

Your date with the cosmos unfolds dramatically, with flamboyance and style. Your need for creative expression is the fuel that propels you to achieve, and action and initiative are the vehicles that get you to where you want to go. Scorpio does much the same thing, but usually without all the drama. Her piercing intuition cuts a clear path toward her goal.

Spiritually, Scorpio lives and breathes at a profound level and as a parent has encouraged you to pursue your dreams from a spiritual foundation.

The Challenge

If, as an adult, you're bewildered by your Scorpio parent's behaviors, attitudes, beliefs and decisions, then the challenge is to figure it out, Leo. The best way to do this is through conversation rather than confrontation, through observation rather than criticism, through calmness rather than hostility.

Virgo Child & Scorpio Parent

Wow!

Generally, this relationship should be comfortable and harmonious. Earth and water, after all, enjoy each other's company. You, Virgo, like your mutable air sign cousin, Gemini, are ruled by Mercury, the planet that governs communication, information and travel. And like Gemini, your steel-trap mind is constantly busy, churning through endless pieces of data, collating details and sculpting them according to some inner blueprint of perfection. It's irrelevant if your Scorpio parent or anyone else has any idea what you're doing. *You* know, and that's all that matters.

Where Gemini collects information and communicates it, you collect information and sift through it for the details that matter and attempt to apply these details in a practical way. In this process, you discriminate every step of the way. Your ideal of perfection is never compromised, and it's this ideal that guides your every action, decision and interest. Even though Scorpio may find your penchant for details bewildering, she admires your ability to connect the dots.

Getting Along

From the time you were a toddler, you exhibited a special gift that you willingly shared with others without any thought of compensation. Scorpio recognized it and helped to nurture and encourage it. Regardless of your age now, your Scorpio parent continues to do that.

The problems that could surface in this relationship are connected to your respective sign rulers. When Mercury, the messenger, comes up against Scorpio's ruler, Pluto, the transformer, or against co-ruler Mars, the warrior, then you encounter your parent's inflexibility and stubbornness. Your reaction to that is a question: *why?* Why can't you go to that outdoor concert? Why can't you have a pet monkey? Why can't you go to college out of state? *Why, why, why* is your litany, your defense and your weapon and evidence of your need to understand.

You can't change this about yourself any more than Scorpio can change the lens through which he perceives himself and the world. So when you come up against Scorpio's implacable rules, collect the facts that support your contention and present them. You can talk circles around virtually anyone, Virgo, but with Scorpio, all the dots have to connect before he'll change his mind.

Simple Guidelines

Harmony is what every child/parent relationship is after, right? Within a harmonious relationship, both people are better able to evolve spiritually, creatively and emotionally. Whether you're living at home or on your own, post this list where you'll see it often.

> ➤ Don't always be the one who gives in when you and Scorpio disagree. As a mutable sign, you're the one most likely to back away from a confrontation. But when you do this consistently, Scorpio becomes entrenched in the idea that he's right, that he knows best and that you'll always do what he wants. Scorpio, after all, must learn to compromise.
> ➤ When you're irritated at Scorpio, ask yourself what the core issue is. It may be that you're annoyed at yourself for something and have projected it onto Scorpio. But if there's a real issue here, then state it. Encourage your parent to discuss it.
> ➤ Don't criticize Scorpio or yourself!

Family Vacations/Reunions with a Scorpio

Family vacations and reunions can be fun, stressful, creative and memorable or complete disasters. As a kid, you were probably just happy to get away from home or to see other family members, so your experiences were invariably fun and memorable. As an adult, much of what you experience depends on your expectations, beliefs and hopes. So before the vacation or reunion, put yourself in a frame of mind that embraces the get-together.

How to Get Your Way

For you, getting your way is actually pretty simple. Gather the details as only a Virgo can, connect them so they form a broad canvas and then present this to Scorpio. You may want to consider writing your parent a letter or an email so that your own thoughts are crystalline.

The Bigger Picture

Even if you didn't have a Scorpio parent, you would delve into mystical realms. You're a natural for this exploration. Your critical thinking and analytical mind, combined with your need to sift through information, enable you to draw on your intuition and to develop a spiritual awareness in this journey. Your Scorpio parent can be of great help in this area. Ask her to join you on the exploration.

The Challenge

If you have unresolved issues with your parents, there's no better time than right now for connecting the dots, scrutinizing the details and figuring out how to resolve it. No one is better equipped than you, Virgo, at details. It's the kind of process you enjoy. So get busy!

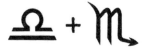

Libra Child & Scorpio Parent

Peacemaker

At heart, you're a mediator, a negotiator, a diplomat and the true peace lover of the zodiac. As a cardinal air sign ruled by Venus, your nature is essentially gentle and artistic, and you have a highly developed aesthetic sense. You're very much a social creature, and your friends are numerous. When you were younger, everyone undoubtedly congregated at your home. If you're a teenager or a college student living at home, your friends probably still come to your place, particularly if you have an area that is all yours—like a finished basement.

Regardless of your age, when you come up against Pluto and Mars, the planets that rule and co-rule Scorpio, you may sometimes feel like racing off into the woods and screaming like a banshee. Or you may simply give in to whatever Scorpio expects or wants so you can avoid a confrontation. This is where issues surface in your relationship with Scorpio.

Getting Along

You long ago mastered the art of social camouflage. Because you usually look like the very paragon of calm, most people can't tell what you're feeling at any given moment. Within you, though, a battle ensues that usually boils down to your most persistent issue: how to maintain harmony without compromising so completely that peace comes at any cost. Your relationship with your Scorpio parent is likely to highlight this issue repeatedly until you've resolved it.

With Scorpio as your parent, you either spend a lifetime bending to his will or you learn to stand up for yourself. It's ironic that a sign connected with balance and harmony has such difficulties with these very qualities. It's due to your reluctance to hurt anyone and to your ability to see the many sides of any issue. You understand where Scorpio is coming from and even though you may disagree, you can live with the paradox. It's your gift. How can you use this gift so that you aren't always the one who gives in, compromises and backs away from confrontation? Read on!

Simple Guidelines

Regardless of your age at this point, post this list where you'll see it often.

> ➢ When you come up against the controlling facet of Scorpio's personality, don't waffle, back down, make excuses or run for the hills. Make your stand, particularly if it's about something important to you. State your case.

- ➢ Explain your bottom line. Scorpio understands bottom lines and will listen closely.
- ➢ Be decisive.

Family Vacations/Reunions with a Scorpio

Whether you're still living at home or are an adult with your own family, vacations and family reunions can be conduits to creativity. You have great, singular focus when your creative passions are ignited, so be sure to take your iPad or a computer along with you to jot down thoughts, feelings or ideas. And bring your iPod. Music soothes you. It's your refuge and your solace and offers what all Libras seek: peace, balance and harmony.

In other words, a vacation or reunion that includes your Scorpio parent can be an adventure into your own creative process. No telling where it may take you.

How to Get Your Way

Diplomacy, tact, mediation and negotiation: these are your tools. Use them with Scorpio as you would use them with anyone else. Don't be indecisive or fearful about using your skills just because Scorpio is your parent and an authority figure. Scorpio is also a human being.

The Bigger Picture

As a cardinal air sign, your approach to spiritual issues is intellectual and often motivated by your questions and concerns about relationships. Perhaps you gather information from books and the Internet and then expand your research through workshops and seminars where you meet other people who hold similar beliefs. You weigh and evaluate what you learn, look at all sides of the issue and then make up your own mind.

Your path in this regard differs from that of your Scorpio parent. She intuits and feels her way along this path. But in the end, your destination is the same. You both uncover and discover your core spiritual beliefs.

The Challenge

Any unresolved issues you have with your Scorpio parent may revolve around feelings you have that you aren't good enough or smart enough or creative enough to achieve what you desire. The irony, though, is that such insecurities are self-created. So, forgive, forget and move on, Libra. You'll be surprised at how quickly the issues are resolved once you do that.

♏ + ♏
Scorpio Child & Scorpio Parent

Intense

Yikes! With this child/parent combination, let's hope that one or both of you have natal moons in an earth sign—Taurus, Virgo, Capricorn—or even in an air sign—Gemini, Libra, Aquarius. An earth sign moon would enable you to take all that intense emotion and funnel it in a practical way. An air sign moon would enable you to talk about those feelings and communicate them verbally. Even a fire sign moon—Aries, Leo, Sagittarius—would be a plus and enable you to externalize your feelings.

Generally, you and your Scorpio parent should get along fine—except when you don't! The latter is most likely to occur over issues concerning control and the balance of power.

Getting Along

Let's say you're under twenty-one, still living at home, work part-time and would like to spend ten days over Christmas break traveling with a friend. Scorpio says, *No way. It's Christmas; you're staying here.* But this trip is really important to you and you're paying for it yourself. So what do you do? Plead your case with the other parent? Blow up? Threaten to run away from home? Refuse to speak to Scorpio ever again?

Well, if you pick any of the above choices, nothing will change. What you do first is put yourself into a meditative state and visualize yourself already on the trip, enjoying it with your friend. Back this visualization with emotion. Imagine the scents in the air, the vivid colors and the sounds. Trust that the trip will happen. Let your intuition guide you about how you should approach Scorpio. Follow through with that guidance.

Regardless of your age, the key to getting along with your Scorpio parent is to treat her the way you want to be treated and to draw on your own intuitive power and skills in your relationship with her.

Simple Guidelines

As a Scorpio child of a Scorpio parent, you may look at the heading for this section and think, *What? There's no such thing as simple in this relationship.* But there actually is because you're both Scorpios.

- ➤ Connect intuitively. You and your Scorpio parent share such a deep psychic bond that you probably pick up on each other's thoughts and feelings quite often. In maintaining harmony in the relationship, begin with your intuitive connection.
- ➤ Enjoy what you have in common. All too often in the child/parent relationship, we forget how to have fun. What do you and your Scorpio parent enjoy doing together? One daughter/mother pair of Scorpios I know go ghost hunting together. A son/father pair are involved in competitive sports.
- ➤ *Know thyself.* Pluto, as ruler of your sign, demands nothing less than a full commitment to this adage. The better you know yourself, the more deeply you understand your Scorpio parent.

Family Vacations/Reunions with a Scorpio

Whether it's a vacation or a reunion, you and your parent are probably on the same page. If you're still living at home, the only conflict that might crop up while you're traveling is about who's in charge and who has the final say. If you're an adult with your own family and you're at a reunion, the question of who's in charge probably won't be an issue. You both are!

How to Get Your Way

If you're living at home and are under the age of twenty-one, then getting your way with a Scorpio parent may be challenging. Ask yourself if what you want is worth a confrontation. Pose the question to yourself out loud. How does it make you feel? The more powerful the emotion, the greater the significance of what you want. If you feel resistance to the question, then it may be wisest to let things alone for a while and trust that the situation will work out to your benefit.

Some battles are worth fighting. Others aren't worth the angst. Let your emotions and intuition guide you in your choice of battles.

The Bigger Picture

For an evolved Scorpio soul, spirituality is the main focus in life. Its manifestation varies, but from the time you were old enough to talk and to begin exploring your world, you sought to unravel every mystery around you—from the mundane to the spectacular. And your Scorpio parent relished—and still does—being a part of this journey.

The Challenge

As an adult, the most likely issue you have with your Scorpio parent is control. Who's in charge? Well, you are, of course. You are the master of your own life and the creator of your own destiny. Once you believe that, you've met the challenge, and the issue between you and mom or dad dissolves on its own.

Sagittarius Child & Scorpio Parent

Why not?

Let's cut to the chase. Unless you and your Scorpio parent have natal moons in compatible signs or other aspects in your respective charts that blend well, this relationship can be difficult. As a mutable fire sign, you're as restless and impatient as Gemini, and are so often in a hurry that you overlook details or shrug them off as unimportant. You're more focused on the big picture and prefer to leave the details to other people. This drives your Scorpio parent nuts.

Your sign is ruled by Jupiter, the planetary giant in our solar system that governs luck, the law, foreign travel, cultures and countries, religion, spirituality, expansion and growth, higher education and the higher mind. As a result of this ruler's influence, you're an exuberant, optimistic individual with an expansive personality. You think big. In contrast, Scorpio is ruled by Pluto, the planet that governs power, the afterlife, death and regeneration, and co-ruled by Mars, the warrior that governs our physicality and sexuality. As a result of these respective rulerships, you may sometimes think your Scorpio parent is morose and way too rigid. And your Scorpio parent may sometimes think you're too swept up in your social life.

Given these differences, how can you find harmony in a relationship with your Scorpio parent?

Getting Along

There are three fundamental things to remember if you want to get along with Scorpio:

- If your parent asks you to do something, don't shrug it off or procrastinate regardless of your age. Do it, and be done with it. Yes, you would rather be out and about having fun, but as long as you're living at home, you have your share of responsibilities.
- Charm gets you only so far. Diplomacy and tact take you the rest of the way. Avoid the biting bluntness that you sometimes resort to—unless you're prepared to experience Scorpio's sting.
- Don't pretend to be knowledgeable in areas you know little or nothing about. Scorpio will call you on it every time.

Your compassionate nature—whether it's for humanitarian causes, the environment, animal and human rights or spiritual freedom—speaks volumes to Scorpio. It's an area you have in common.

Simple Guidelines

Your sign's image is that of the centaur—half horse, half man. In a sense, it represents the two sides of your personality—the buoyant charmer and compassionate Sadge who is always seeking the larger picture, and the Sadge who can be selfish and self-centered, a boastful know-it-all. When dealing with Scorpio, strive for the compassionate charmer. Here are some other tips for maintaining harmony with your Scorpio parent:

- Value your freedom and the independence that Scorpio helps to foster in you.
- Don't always be the one to compromise. Mutable signs tend to give in during a confrontation with a fixed sign. That said, you're also a fire sign who won't compromise your integrity and will rebel if someone attempts to impose unreasonable restrictions on you.
- Always stand up for what you believe in—even if those beliefs differ from Scorpio's.

Family Vacations/Reunions with a Scorpio

This is where conflict may surface. At heart, you're a nomad, and this quality has been evident since you were really young. So if your Scorpio parent plans a family vacation with a rigid schedule, you'll be the first to voice a complaint. And if Scorpio refuses to take your complaint under consideration, you'll find some way to make the vacation an adventure to remember.

Once you're an adult and are preparing to embark on one of your quests for truth, which often involves travel to some far-flung part of the world, invite Scorpio to go along. She'll surprise you with her ability to ferret out the very secrets you're looking for, and suddenly, you see each other in an entirely new and different light.

How to Get Your Way

Since you can be mentally oriented when it suits you, use your logic and passion to convince Scorpio that your way is the right way!

The Bigger Picture

With Jupiter as your ruler, you have a natural interest in spiritual and philosophical issues. But there are two types of Sadges in this regard: the religious fanatic and the spiritual pioneer.

The first type gets locked into a narrow expression of spirituality because he believes his way is the only way, and bludgeons others with his point of view. The second type is the true seeker. His spiritual beliefs may involve foreign cultures—gurus in India or the study of mythology in some remote part of the planet. Even astral travel may interest him.

Guess which type finds the greatest companionship with Scorpio?

The Challenge

As an adult, any issues you have with your Scorpio parent probably involve your personal freedom. Perhaps you were told "No" so often when you were a kid that the "NO" loop is still playing in your head. *NO, you can't do that. NO, you can't go there. NO, that's too dangerous.* The challenge for you is to break that loop. The next time you're about to tell yourself "NO," say "YES" instead. When you do this often enough, the old loop will start falling apart.

Capricorn Child & Scorpio Parent

Dependable

For you, Capricorn, life is about responsibility, rules, parameters, goals, achievement and hard work. You're a serious-minded person who sometimes strikes other people as aloof and reserved. At times, you can be as emotionally reserved—and as secretive—as your Scorpio parent. These traits are partly due to the planet that rules your sign, Saturn. It governs discipline, responsibility, obedience, structure and foundations. No wonder you're the workhorse of the zodiac!

Getting Along

For the most part, this child/parent combination works well. There's a nice balance of energies, and you and Scorpio possess an almost instinctive understanding of how the other thinks and feels. If you're in your early teens, you probably don't even mind the structures and rules that Scorpio has in place. However, as you mature through high school, college and beyond, you may rebel against the rules. Outright rebellion isn't your style, so you'll find a subtle way of letting your Scorpio parent know that some rules are intended to be bent. And you'll be blunt in asking Scorpio why her way is the correct way.

Simple Guidelines

This relationship works well enough so that most of the time just being who you are is enough to keep the peace with your Scorpio parent. But when you encounter bumps and setbacks, here are some tips for re-establishing harmony:

> ➢ Don't brood or react with silence. Engage Scorpio in a discussion about whatever is going on, and do so without anger or rancor.
> ➢ Be alert for synchronicities that may provide insight and guidance.
> ➢ Go the gym, take a yoga class or go hiking. Physical activity is a great outlet for you and removes you temporarily from the situation. You return with a fresh perspective.

Family Vacations/Reunions with a Scorpio

A vacation planned by your Scorpio parent suits you just fine. However Scorpio structures it, you're probably okay with it. You like knowing where you're going to be and when and what you're going to see. Chances are, you helped organize the vacation and built in some latitude so there's time for side trips where any sort of adventure may occur.

If you're an adult with a family of your own and are vacationing with your parents, it's likely that you're calling the shots and planning the itinerary. Scorpio may balk, but by now, you're accustomed to seizing the helm.

How to Get Your Way

Getting your way with your Scorpio parent may be easier than you think. Present what you want in terms of a goal you would like to achieve. Let's say you would like to take horseback riding lessons, but your Scorpio parent has said no because lessons and all the gear you need are too expensive. You should present horseback riding as something you would like to learn how to do, and you'll help pay for it with what you earn from your part-time job. You've also researched the price of gear and have found everything you need on Craigslist for a fraction of what it all costs new.

Now you're speaking Scorpio's language!

The Bigger Picture
Your need for structure may play into your approach to spiritual issues. If you follow an organized religion, then you do it with full commitment and involvement. If you follow a nontraditional course, then it's likely you establish your own parameters. The point is to somehow use your spiritual explorations to deepen your understanding of yourself. Regardless of the course you choose, your Scorpio parent is supportive.

The Challenge
As an adult, any issues you have with your Scorpio parent can be easily resolved by doing what you have always done when you want something: define your goal, lay out your strategy for attaining it and then go for it.

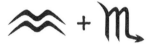

Aquarius Child & Scorpio Parent

Rebel
In many ways, you're the wild card of the zodiac, individualistic, innovative and a rebel and anarchist at heart. Your sign ushers in new ideas, new paradigms and unique ways of doing things. You're the humanitarian and are deeply compassionate and concerned about equality and fairness in all things. You don't recognize social barriers, and at every opportunity, you attempt to reform rigid conventions.

As an Aquarian, the energy you brought into life with you may be the kind of energy that was lacking in your family before you arrived. If your family is prejudiced, you break through that prejudice. If your family isn't concerned about humanitarian causes, you change that. For a Scorpio parent, you're a handful.

Getting Along

As a fixed air sign, you're just as stubborn as Scorpio, and when you two come up against each other's inability to compromise, it's not pretty. A look at the respective rulers of your signs may offer clues about how to get along.

Uranus, ruler of Aquarius, governs individuality, genius, eccentricity, breaks with tradition and disruptions to old patterns. Like Neptune and Pluto, the ruler of Scorpio, it's considered to be a transcendental planet that can be dealt with constructively only through an expanded consciousness. So let's start there, with the idea of expanded consciousness.

Neither you nor Scorpio accepts something as true just because an expert or authority figure says it is. Scorpio delves and digs until he finds the bottom line. You study and research something until you find its core truth. Scorpio's approach is emotional and intuitive and yours is intellectual. There's common ground here to build on.

Simple Guidelines

One sure way to maintain harmony in your relationship with Scorpio is by sharing your varied creative projects with him. Draw him in. Listen to his ideas. Engage him in the process, and don't be surprised when he reciprocates in the same way. Here are some other tips:

> ➢ Don't become so entrenched in your own ideas and beliefs that you stop listening to anything Scorpio says. Maintain your sense of curiosity.

- Don't withhold emotionally. Give your Scorpio parent a bear hug daily! By doing this, you're not just communicating your feelings to Scorpio, but are also connecting with a deep place within yourself.
- Always ask yourself: What is my myth? What myth am I living? What myth would I like to live? And then ask yourself the same questions about Scorpio. To a large extent, emotions define our "bliss," what author and mythologist Joseph Campbell called living the "mythologically inspired life."

Family Vacations/Reunions with a Scorpio

Depending on your age, a family vacation with your Scorpio parent may be something you hope to avoid—*unless* the destination is a place that intrigues you. And then you'll happily go along with whatever agenda Scorpio has established as long as you have the freedom to explore once you arrive.

If you're an adult attending a family reunion that includes your Scorpio parent, whatever issues you have probably are left at home. After all, it's just a reunion, and you live by your own rules and code now.

How to Get Your Way

When you want something that's important to you and Scorpio stands in your way of getting it, whatever it is, do what you do best: think outside the box. Figure out a solution that will work for you and Scorpio. Gather your facts, prepare your case and when you're ready, present your argument to Scorpio.

If that doesn't work, don't threaten to run away from home. Return to your drawing board, and come up with another way to win your case.

The Bigger Picture

Your friends and even some of your acquaintances are often important for more than just companionship and camaraderie. They can also be key to your spiritual development through exchanges of ideas, concepts and communication. So when you insist on having the gang over to your house for the weekend, Scorpio may not always be thrilled with it, but she understands that at the core of all this it's important in your spiritual evolution.

The Challenge

As an adult, the challenge for you, Aquarius, is to not allow estrangement between yourself and your Scorpio parent. This challenge may be especially difficult if Scorpio sought to control you during your teen years when you were just discovering what rebellion meant. Remember: love is the strongest force in the universe.

Pisces Child & Scorpio Parent

Dreamer

You're the true mystic of the zodiac—sensitive, moody, imaginative and as psychic as your Scorpio parent. Your ability enables you to delve into the unconscious river of knowledge that unites all people, and when you surface from that place, your imagination spins tales about what you experienced. Scorpio tends to use her psychic ability to further her own knowledge and to connect telepathically with the people she loves.

The rulers of your respective signs hold significant clues about how you each use your ability. Your sign, Pisces, is ruled by Neptune, one of the outer, transcendental planets. In its least desirable manifestation, Neptune breaks rules by creating confusion, vagueness and escapism. In its most evolved manifestation, Neptune brings great imagination, creativity and spiritual depth. Most Pisces exhibit both sides of the Neptunian influence.

Scorpio is ruled by Pluto, also an outer, transcendental planet. It represents transformation at the deepest levels—death and rebirth, destruction and power. Pluto is never ambivalent or passive. It enables Scorpio to tap into the collective mind in all its hypnotizing horror and magnificent beauty. In a sense, you and Scorpio are able to arrive at the same place, but what you take away from that collective energy and how you use it differs.

Getting Along

You and Scorpio actually get along well. You're both water signs who view the world and yourselves through the lens of your emotions and intuition. Your telepathic connection is so strong that you may finish each other's sentences. The risk for you, Pisces, is that you're so receptive to other people's energies that you may be overwhelmed at times by Scorpio's intensity and will need to put some distance between you.

You're exceptionally compatible when it comes to anything creative. Where Scorpio intuits her way through her creativity, you create in an organic, holistic way, intuitively perceiving the entirety of what you're trying to create. This is true whether you're cooking for twenty-five or writing a screenplay. When you and Scorpio combine forces on any creative or artistic project, the result is likely to be magnificent.

Simple Guidelines

As a mutable water sign, you're emotionally adaptable. This trait makes it difficult for you to pin down exactly what you feel at any given moment. Are you happy right now or are you just saying you are because it's what someone else wants to hear? This kind of emotional ambivalence could be a bone of contention between you and Scorpio because it often prompts you to change your mind. *I'll be there for dinner at 6:00* becomes *Can we make it breakfast tomorrow?* It may seem like a small thing to you, but it isn't to Scorpio. Try to carry through when you make dates and appointments.

Here are some other tips for keep your relationship with Scorpio at an even keel:

➢ When dealing with your Scorpio parent, try to strike a balance between what your intuition and your intellect tell you.
➢ Don't be a pushover and always give in to what Scorpio wants. This may be tough to do since your parent is an authority figure, but the learning curve in this relationship is mutual.
➢ When in doubt about how to deal with Scorpio, summon your muse, and find a creative solution!

Family Vacations/Reunions with a Scorpio

Water sign individuals often have a thing about being near water—a swimming pool, pond, lake, river, sea and better yet, an ocean. So with at least two water signs in your family, suggest renting a cabin on a river, lake or at the beach for the family vacation or reunion. The proximity to a body of water soothes both you and Scorpio, boosts your physical and psychic energy and enables you to relax into nature.

How to Get Your Way

First, make sure that what you want is *really* what you want. Commit to it. Then spend a few minutes each day imagining yourself discussing it with Scorpio and your parent agreeing that, yes, this would be a great thing for you to have/do. The trick lies in backing this visualization with emotion and imagining that you already have whatever it is you want. It has to be real for you, already *tangible*.

Once you feel you've already gotten whatever it is that you want and you have seen, in your head, how Scorpio agrees to this, then approach your parent with the idea. If you have made your visualization compelling, vivid, detailed and emotionally real, then it's likely you'll get what you want. It's not magic. By combining your intentions and desire with powerful emotion, the universe responds.

The Bigger Picture

You and Scorpio selected each other for these particular roles in this lifetime and, at some level, you're both aware of it. Perhaps, from you, Scorpio is supposed to learn to lighten up, to ignite his imagination and allow it to whisk him away. From Scorpio, perhaps you're supposed to learn to stand up for yourself and avoid the martyr/savior syndrome that some Pisces experience. Or maybe Scorpio teaches you how to maintain a sense of yourself during any transformative experience.

Whatever the dynamics of your relationship in this life, you are teachers and mentors for each other.

The Challenge

As an adult the challenge for you, Pisces, is greater independence from your Scorpio parent. Because you're both water signs and deeply intuitive, you're attuned to each other. You may feel that even now Scorpio is peering over your shoulder, judging what you do and don't do. Banish that inner censor. Nothing can be further from the truth. Scorpio applauds your independence.

Chapter 5:

The Enigma of Your Scorpio Kid

"Scorpio is the only sign that never produces a shallow person."
- Astrologer Grant Lewi

Intense, passionate, fearless. These adjectives are often used to describe a Scorpio child, but they barely scratch the surface. These kids are complex and mysterious and often a complete enigma to the people who love and know them best. And it begins the moment they draw their first breath.

As a parent, look back to the birth of your Scorpio child. Were there any unusual events surrounding the child's birth? Was he born before or after his due date? Synchronicity often occurs during major transitions in our lives—and a birth certainly qualifies as a major event. Can you recall any meaningful coincidences that happened? Does your partner or another family member recall anything unusual? Was the birth easy or difficult?

In a young group of her peers, the Scorpio child is easy to spot—she's the solitary brooder, the one with the soulful eyes who appears to be lost in her own thoughts. She's actually checking out everything around her quite carefully and has learned to do this without seeming to do so. If Scorpio joins in the activities, it's with a few close friends who are as loyal to her as she is to them.

Early on, you'll notice your Scorpio child's potent emotions, which are her primary vehicle for exploring the world. Unlike her water sign cousins, Cancer and Pisces, the driving intensity of these emotions can sometimes overpower other children. And at times, they can overwhelm you, too. The best way to deal with it is to allow your Scorpio to experience the full range of her emotions and encourage her to talk about what she feels.

Scorpio blows only when he's pushed to the absolute edge, so these emotional outbursts aren't temper tantrums. He simply needs some help understanding why he feels things so deeply while other kids go on their merry way.

Emotional release for a Scorpio child can be found through any creative outlet—art, music, writing, photography, gardening. Many Scorpio children have so much innate talent that they don't need formal lessons to play an instrument or to draw or paint. They're naturals. They pick up a paintbrush, and off they go. Or they sit down at a piano and play even if they can't read a note of music.

Intuition/Creativity & Your Scorpio Child

Since many Scorpios seem to be born intuitive, these kids enjoy games in which they must use their intuition. One game that Scorpio might enjoy involves telepathy. In this game, one of you acts as the sender and the other is the receiver. The sender should think of a color and make the visualization as vivid and bold as possible—instead of just visualizing red, make it *scarlet*. The receiver should sit quietly with his eyes shut, mind a blank and say the first color that pops into his head. With a little practice, the results may astonish you.

Past Lives

Scorpio kids often bring in an awareness and memories of their past lives. You'll know this is the case if your young child has an inordinate interest in something specific—like WWII airplanes, vintage cars or a particular city or geographic location or even a particular house in your neighborhood. These past-life memories usually begin to fade by the age of five or six, about the time your child starts school.

In *Children's Past Lives*, author and past-life therapist Carol Bowman details the specifics she has found in young children who apparently have recalled their previous lives. Usually, the life has an emotional connection to the current life, a similar theme or lesson that must be learned and/or communicated.

When you've mastered one role, switch things around. The sender becomes the receiver and vice versa. If Scorpio's intuition isn't discouraged by religious beliefs or superstitions, it can easily develop into psychic ability.

If your Scorpio child is in middle school or high school and already has his own cell phone, there's an app called ESP Trainer that's a wonderful tool for developing intuition. It was developed under a NASA program by author and researcher Russell Targ at Stanford Research Institute. The app randomly generates a color photo beneath one of the four squares on the screen and you must use your intuitive ability to choose the right square. Each set consists of twenty-four trials, and your ESP score is based on how many correct choices you make.

The app has positive feedback built into it. From the website: "When you succeed, you will hear a chime, feel a vibration and see a large colored picture. Otherwise, the system lights up the correct square, and you proceed with the next trial. The score indicator at the top counts the number of correct choices. Words of encouragement appear as you achieve the scoring levels of six, eight, ten, twelve or fourteen hits. After twenty-four trials you may begin a new game."

The game also offers feedback and reinforcement. If you're uncertain about which square to choose, you have the option of passing. As Scorpio becomes more familiar with ESP Trainer, her ability to recognize intuitive impressions will improve. "The purpose of the trainer is to allow you to become aware of what it feels like when you psychically choose the correct square. When you don't have that special feeling, we encourage you to press the Pass button."

The website notes that in a yearlong NASA study with the ESP Trainer, 145 participants were able to significantly improve their scores. Once your Scorpio child starts using this app, just watch how quickly her enthusiasm for it spills over into the rest of the family!

When creativity begins as an emotional release for Scorpio, she quickly discovers her passion for self-expression and often taps into a particular area that speaks to her soul. It might be painting or writing, photography, music, dance or some other type of artistic pursuit. It could be some unique combination of all of the above or even something that integrates art and the paranormal. Or, equally possible, your Scorpio child may discover he has a talent for telepathy or out of body travel.

Years ago when I taught Spanish to hormonal seventh graders, I used to reserve one class a week for experiments and discussions about psychic phenomena—in English. It was something the kids had to earn—if they behaved the other four days, then they won the psi bonus day. There were several Scorpios in the class who had zero interest in Spanish but really rallied on those bonus days. It was as if they had lived their first twelve or thirteen years with an entire portion of their personalities split off from ordinary life, and now, suddenly, they had an opportunity to talk about some of their experiences.

These Scorpio kids excelled at everything we tried—reading auras, dream recall, telepathy. One Scorpio boy began having out of body experiences (OBEs) and told his parents about it. His mother equated OBEs with an aberrant mental condition and expressed her concern to me. I tried to explain it to her, but realized she just didn't understand. So I stopped talking about OBEs in class, and the Scorpio kid and I confined our discussions to after-school hours.

He taught me something important about Scorpio children: always listen to them even if they're talking about stuff that is not within your field of knowledge. You never know what may develop, as author and researcher Carol Bowman discovered with her Scorpio son, Chase.

Chase's Story

On July 4, 1988, Carol, her husband, Steve, five-year-old Chase and their nine-year-old daughter, Sarah, headed for the golf course near their home in Asheville, North Carolina, to watch the fireworks display. Chase usually loved the fireworks, but as the cannon-like booms reverberated through the air, Chase suddenly began to cry. Carol asked him what was wrong, but he just wailed harder and louder. As Carol tried to calm him down, his sobs grew into hysteria, and she realized she needed to get him away from the fireworks, so she took him home. He continued to sob, and Carol held him in her lap in a rocking chair on the front porch until he finally fell asleep.

His hysteria that night bewildered her. Chase had never before been afraid of fireworks. In fact, Chase wasn't easily frightened by anything. She wrote it off as the long day and too much excitement. But a month later, the hysteria happened again when Carol and Chase had gone to a friend's house to go swimming. "As soon as he entered the pool area, where the sound of the diving board and splashing and yelling echoed in the big hall, he began to cry hysterically," wrote Carol in *Children's Past Lives*. "Howling and screaming, he grabbed my arm with both hands and dragged me toward the door."

A few weeks later, Carol and her family had a houseguest, Norman Inge, a skilled hypnotherapist. He was staying with the Bowmans while he conducted workshops in Asheville on past-life regressions. One afternoon, Carol, her two kids and Norman were sitting around the kitchen table, listening to Norman's stories. Carol thought about Chase's irrational fear of loud noises and told Norman about it. He asked Chase if he would like to try an experiment. "That moment, I realized later, was a turning point in my life. Up to that time I had never thought that children could remember their past lives," Carol wrote.

Norman asked Chase to sit in Carol's lap, shut his eyes and describe what he saw when he could hear the loud noises. Chase began describing himself as a soldier, and the description fit that of the Civil War. "I'm behind a rock," Chase said. "I don't want to look, but I have to when I shoot. Smoke and flashes everywhere. And loud noises: yelling, screaming and loud booms. I'm not sure who I'm shooting at—there's so much smoke, so much going on. I'm scared. I shoot at anything that moves. I really don't want to be here and shoot other people."

Chase was struck in the right wrist by a bullet and was taken off the battlefield to a first-aid tent where his wrist was bandaged. Sarah realized that spot on his wrist was where Chase had had eczema since he was a baby. But within a few days of the regression to that lifetime, the eczema disappeared and Chase's fear of loud noises vanished completely and never returned.

This regression was pivotal for Carol and for Chase. Over the course of the next three years, she trained in hypnotherapy and studied past-life regression techniques with Norman and with Dr. Roger Woolger. Her life path had been dramatically changed by the experience, and Chase was free of his debilitating fear.

Then in 1991, the conflict in Iraq broke out and the first Scud missile attack on Israel occurred. The day after the war began, Carol picked up Chase from school and he announced: "They'll never make me fight again!" Chase told Carol he wanted to do another regression like he'd had with Norman. Carol realized that all the talk at school about the war had triggered Chase's memories of that Civil War life, and she agreed to regress him. In this regression, Carol learned that Chase had been a free black man. When he'd gone back to the battlefield with his bandaged hand, he'd been shot by a cannon and killed.

Carol eventually went on to study with Dr. Ian Stevenson, a psychiatrist at the University of Virginia who was one of the few Westerners to study children's past lives. She began regressing Chase's friends, collecting data about children's past lives. She wrote an article for *Mothering* magazine and began planning a book on the subject. But in 1993, Carol's husband was downsized out of his job, and the money he was making as a consultant was barely enough to sustain the family. Carol realized she needed to put her book idea on hold and get a real job.

In mid-February of that year, she walked around her neighborhood and struggled to accept that her research and the book had to be abandoned. "I conceded to the sullen sky that if I were meant to write the book on children's past life memories, I would need a miracle to make it happen," she wrote.

When she got home, she sat on the front porch, numb with despair. Steve suddenly burst through the door with the phone in hand, and punched a key on the telephone to replay the voice-mail. "This is the Oprah Winfrey show in Chicago calling for Carol Bowman. Could you please call me back right away?"

"In a flash," Carol wrote, "I grasped the full meaning of this call. I had gotten my miracle."

Carol, Chase and Sarah were guests on Oprah's show with several other mothers and their children, including a mother who had written to the Oprah show nearly a year earlier about Carol's work. As a result of their appearance on the show, Carol wrote her book and sold it to Bantam Books. *Children's Past Lives* was followed by *Return from Heaven* some years later, and Carol is now a full-time past-life therapist who is booked months in advance. Chase, now in his early thirties, is a videographer who travels worldwide.

Their respective life paths, the core of their creative talents, might have turned out much differently if Carol hadn't listened to her Scorpio son's profound and crippling fear that hot July night in 1988.

Scorpio Child's Life Stages

As the parent of a Scorpio, you probably realize that every phase of your child's life is marked by unusual events or experiences that underscore just how special this kid is. You may never understand the full scope of his personality, of what motivates and drives him, but you'll see evidence of it.

Infancy to Seven

Way before your Scorpio starts school, you'll have some idea of the energy this child has brought into life with him. His charisma is apparent right from the start and draws people of all ages—from doting grandmothers to young kids. Your Scorpio son or daughter even attracts household pets!

One thing you'll notice early on is that your child takes life seriously. Even before he can talk, there's something in his gaze that is watchful, eerily observant. You might find him lying quietly in his crib, for example, fixated on a colorful mobile or at the play of shadows on the ceiling. His rapt attention might tempt you to stretch out on the floor alongside his crib and study whatever he's looking at.

This same focused attention is evident when he begins to crawl and walk. He explores his space carefully, taking in the details, learning the lay of the land, moving always at his own measured pace. If you have pets, it won't be uncommon for the family cat or dog to join him in his explorations.

When Scorpio begins talking, it's unlikely that he'll be a chatterbox, unless he has a pronounced air sign influence in his chart, like a Gemini moon or rising. He uses language carefully and precisely. He benefits from daycare or some kind of pre-K schooling where he's with other kids engaged in group activities. This early socialization urges him out of his intense self-containment.

In school, the friendships he forges are rarely frivolous or quick. He isn't the sort of kid who walks up to a complete stranger and instantly offers a *Reader's Digest* version of who he is. His approach to other kids is as measured and diligent as his early explorations were. He withholds a part of himself until the other person has won his loyalty and trust.

Even as early as kindergarten, he's a conscientious student, but may be more interested in art, music, PE and sports than he is in the three Rs. Once he hits elementary school, though, you'll have a good idea where his skills and interests lie. The focus and concentration that marks your child from an early age is usually on display in the classroom and makes him a favorite among his teachers.

Seven to Fourteen

Scorpio's thrust for independence during this period usually occurs on a deep, unconscious level and may manifest itself as stubbornness, nightmares, dreams of flying or perhaps even a confession that she has—or had—an imaginary friend.

During this period, she also has a lot of questions about weighty issues. *Do animals have souls? Where do we go when we die? Have I lived before? What is God?* And there will be questions about sexuality. Close to the onset of puberty, she may experiment with sex.

Rules must be established before this stage, so that your Scorpio child understands how things work at home and in the outer world. But if you impose strict rules or stringent restrictions on her freedom, expect her to rebel. Since this sign produces some of the most stubborn individuals in the zodiac, many Scorpio children simply won't do what you tell them to do if they feel it's unreasonable. Even threats won't make them budge. So be prepared to explain why you've imposed a particular restriction and why she should do what you've asked. *Why, why, why* will be a familiar litany during this phase.

With any sign, a seven-year-old is a vastly different creature than a young teen. But with a Scorpio child, it's the young teen years that may turn you gray before your time. Around the age of twelve—when your Scorpio enters seventh grade—you'll notice a distinct difference in personality, interests and focus.

She may become more meticulous about her appearance, clothes and hairstyle. She may not like the way you've decorated her room and will insist on more autonomy about her personal space. You may question her choice of friends. Even though Scorpios tend to select their friends carefully and generally don't bend to peer pressure, middle school can be brutal.

The best way to handle these several years is through open communication. Encourage her to talk about her feelings, her school life and her concerns. If you notice that she's moodier than usual or more withdrawn, ask her if she'd like to talk about it. Also, do things as a family. Go camping. Travel somewhere Scorpio is eager to see and explore. As self-sufficient as your Scorpio child may be, it's comforting for a young teen to be assured that she has the support and love of her family.

Another excellent outlet for young Scorpio teens is exercise—through sports, a gym, rock climbing, jogging or long walks. If your Scorpio is a loner, then she may prefer solitary activities. Whatever it is, she needs to enjoy the activity. Once it becomes part of her daily routine, she will become more aware of her physicality, nutrition and diet. She'll be more self-assured.

Fourteen to Twenty-One

Bottom line? This phase may get worse before it gets better. Most parents probably feel this way about teenagers, but one parent with a Scorpio son remarked, "At times, I feel like abdicating from the family. Other times, I know I'm blessed." Either/or, black or white: that's how it often is with a Scorpio child. And this stage usually emphasizes the extremes.

Even after you get through the middle school years, high school looms ahead. But somewhere around his sophomore or junior year, at the age of fifteen or sixteen, Scorpio begins to come into his own. He has processed and internalized the lessons of middle school, and his self-sufficiency and self-confidence help him move through the rough spots and challenges he may face.

By this age, if not before, Scorpio has found his creative passion and pursues it with a relentlessness that characterizes this sign. He might have a part-time job and could be saving his money for something special—a seminar or workshop that will expand his talent and creative passion. Or perhaps he's saving money for a car or for a trip somewhere. One thing is certain: his sense of privacy (secrecy?) is now so ingrained that you won't know about the workshop or the trip until he shows you the ticket!

By the age of seventeen or eighteen, when Scorpio graduates from high school and is preparing to embark on the next phase of his journey—college, vocational school, a job or whatever that next step is—you'll have a clearer sense of who your child is. But unless you're also a Scorpio or are exceptionally intuitive, you won't ever know the full story about this child.

Even with the people to whom he's closest, he only reveals parts of himself. He's like the proverbial iceberg in that only a tenth of him is visible to others. The rest is hidden, kept under wraps. In the event that you call his attention to this fact, he'll give you an odd look, flash a winning smile and say something like, "Really?" Or he'll make some humorous crack that diverts your attention from what you just said.

If he leaves home at the age of eighteen, you're going to feel his absence profoundly. Granted, parents initially feel that void when their kids leave home. But when a Scorpio child departs, all of that mysterious energy, that sardonic humor and charisma are also gone. You may walk around your home feeling directionless and bewildered by how your Scorpio grew up so quickly and how the years have flown by.

But if, as a parent, you've done your job and have surrounded your Scorpio with love and encouraged his independence, he'll be home for holidays, maybe even a weekend now and then. And like ET, he'll call home.

Twenty-One & Beyond

Legally, your Scorpio child is now on her own and is embarked on her path, whatever it may be. If she has always known what she wanted to do with her life, then she probably is fully immersed in that passion. If she's still in the process of discovery (unlikely), then she's committed to this quest and is savoring a little of this, a little of that. If she's floundering, then she may be moving from one job and relationship to another.

One of my daughter's closest friends, Ashley, is a Scorpio. She and Megan met in high school, when both attended a dramatic arts charter school in our area. She has that Scorpio magnetism—a piercing gaze, a smile that can light up the dark side of the moon, a sense of humor that can be bitingly sarcastic when the situation calls for it and a spectrum of talents. Even when she was fourteen, she radiated wisdom, as though she were an old soul in a young woman's body.

Ashley's self-sufficiency has always been evident. She completed two years of college while holding down a full-time job but got so burned out that she quit college and went to work for the company where her mother was employed. She was paid well and started saving money for tuition in order to go back to college.

When the company went belly up and her parents moved to Florida's west coast, Ashley remained behind and found another job. At the time, her younger sister was involved in an abusive relationship, got pregnant and eventually left the man. She and her young child moved in with Ashley. For months, Ashley shouldered more than her share of responsibility, acting as a mother to both her sister and her niece.

One night at a party, Ashley witnessed the death of a friend who had had too much to drink and fell off a tenth floor balcony. For the next year, she turned to traditional religion, struggling to find answers to why this had happened, what the larger implications were and how God and faith fit into this picture.

Several years ago, Ashley fell in love with a man whose family is Egyptian and Muslim. A wedding was planned. She asked Megan to be her maid of honor. Then Ashley discovered she was pregnant and the wedding was delayed, but she and the man were married in a Muslim ceremony. Ashley quit her job and went to work for her husband's father, a veterinarian who recently had opened a diagnostic center that did blood work for local veterinary clinics. She worked twelve-hour days, and money was tight. She and her husband had to move in with his parents. The living situation was intolerable for her. Her father-in-law tried to run her life.

Not long after her daughter was born, the center closed down, and the marriage fell apart. Ashley returned to her previous employer, who gladly hired her back with a substantial raise. She plans to return to college in the fall and doesn't yet know what her major will be. But she's adamant that it will be *her* choice, no one else's, and that she'll be calling the shots about the direction of her life from here on in.

When we saw her over the Thanksgiving holidays, she had her six-month-old daughter with her. At twenty-five, she's a self-sufficient single mother who has experienced great contrasts that have helped her define what she hopes to do with the rest of her life. When I asked her about her ex, she rolled her eyes. "No second chances," she replied.

Spoken like a true Scorpio. It's often said that Scorpios never forget or forgive. They just get even. Once the trust is broken, that's it. Scorpio walks away without apologies or regrets.

From the Parent of a Scorpio Son

My sister, Mary, has three sons—the oldest and youngest are Capricorns, as is she, and the middle son, Avery, is a Scorpio. He has been an enigma to her, to all of us, since he sped into the world in what must have been a record delivery time—just a few hours. It was as if Avery was eager to be born, to get on with it and to do whatever he had come here to do.

During family reunions over the years, Avery was always the quiet kid, solitary and observant with his large mahogany-colored eyes taking in everything, missing nothing. Sometimes, I could almost feel his penetrating questions: *Who are you guys? Why am I here? Where did I come from? Where am I going?* None of this was ever verbalized. The questions he asked were his and his alone.

As a kid, Avery never made waves. It's true even now that he's the young man of twenty-four. When he was in college, his car broke down, and he couldn't afford to get it fixed. He knew his mother—divorced by then from his father—was struggling financially, so he didn't ask her for help. He rode a bike to his classes and his job. He didn't complain, didn't let Mary—or even his brothers—know what he was doing. His self-containment has always been like that. As my sister once remarked, "He's a solitary human being who really doesn't need other people."

I asked Mary what it was like to be the mother of a Scorpio son and she kindly consented to write up her impressions about Avery:

> As a baby, he was the easiest of my three sons. He was always happy, a good sleeper. When it got close to his bedtime, he would hold up his arms and stare at me with those big brown eyes and say, "Night-night."

> One of my friends used to joke about his curiosity. She was afraid he would disassemble her car because he wanted to know how it worked. He has always been curious about how things work.

> Typically, Avery was very obedient. He would do whatever I requested. But he had a rebellious/stubborn streak, for sure. One time in a tae kwon do lesson, his instructor told him to do something, and he flat-out refused. It was a contest of wills. Avery stared this guy down, then had to stand over in the corner while the class went on.

He is honest and trustworthy—you can count on him—and he will always do the right thing. The flip side is that he's a dreamer and sometimes isn't focused on the task at hand. You have to get his full attention when speaking to him—he can't be watching TV or be otherwise distracted. He's very much a thinker, always learning and watches mostly educational stuff on TV while I watch trash!

He's very much a loner and has gotten more so over the years. Even athletic activities for which he has a passion are done solo (biking, hiking, running, working out). He spends a lot of time alone. With his peers, he can be awkward in social situations but is a terrific conversationalist with adults.

Recently, he bought a Prius, and I had no idea he was buying a car. He researched for months, looked at the car at a dealership the weekend before, took it to a garage and had them check out everything. Then he bought it the following weekend and came home in the Prius. Very quiet, determined and headstrong. But also very tender hearted.

He is wise beyond his years...an old soul.

Kids with a Scorpio Moon or Scorpio Rising

Throughout the years that I've studied and written about astrology, I've found that kids with a Scorpio moon or Scorpio rising often exhibit traits that are similar to children with a sun in Scorpio. Astrologically, this makes sense.

The moon rules our inner lives, our emotions, intuition, our capacity to nurture and be nurtured and our experience of Mom or our most nurturing parent. Vedic astrologers actually consider the moon and its twenty-seven constellations—called the lunar mansions—as the primary source of predictive techniques.

Your rising sign is how others see you and often dictates your physical appearance. It's why people with Scorpio rising may have that same piercing gaze that individuals with Scorpio suns do and why they tackle many of the same themes and challenges. Your rising sign is also the doorway to your astrological blueprint, the point where you entered this life, and in that context, it may be more important than your sun sign. Some people live out their potential through their moon or rising signs.

Let's say you have a child with a Gemini sun who just doesn't seem to fit the descriptions you read about that sign. She's an introvert whose interests span the spectrum of weirdness, a loner who may be an information junkie, as Gemini kids generally are, but the information she culls is specific to some esoteric bottom line that eludes you. Instead of the chatterbox that a Gemini sun is supposed to be, your child is cocooned in silence, privacy and secrecy. Instead of duality, your kid is a total mystery. It's because this Gemini child is living through her Scorpio moon or rising.

If you know the exact time your child was born, you can obtain a free natal at http://alabe.com/freechart. This website also provides an interpretation for the chart.

Some of the traits of a Scorpio moonchild are similar to those of a child with a Scorpio sun. But since the moon governs our inner lives, there are also marked differences. A child with a Scorpio moon fits the adage: *Still waters run deep.* Beneath all that stillness lies a rich inner life that you, as a parent, may not be privy to. And that inner life begins with her very first breath.

As a youngster, her greatest challenge comes from herself, from her passionate emotions, the way she *feels*. Scorpio moon kids are even less likely to trust a friend than kids with a Scorpio sun, so it's important that when she's young she knows she can confide in you, her parent. And always encourage her to talk about her feelings.

When this child makes a friend, it's because the friend has won her trust. If that trust is broken at any point, the Scorpio moonchild won't forgive and forget. "When someone violates my trust, that's it," remarked a woman with a Scorpio moon. "I simply cut that person out of my life."

Scorpio moon kids, like their adult counterparts, often have a biting sarcasm that emerges when they're hurt or feel threatened. It's a defense mechanism, but when you're on the receiving end of it, you just want to distance yourself from it. As a parent, you can teach this child when sarcasm is inappropriate, but it's unlikely you'll ever eradicate it from her personality.

One thing you can't avoid with this child is honesty about sex. Sexual feelings and experiences are simply a part of this moon sign. If you're open and honest about sexuality and sexual issues and create a loving environment for your child, then some of the adolescent perils can be mitigated.

The Scorpio moon kid may have more obsessive edges to her personality than a child with a Scorpio sun. This can manifest itself as a need to control and manipulate others or a need to get even with people who hurt her. That symbol for Scorpio—the scorpion—speaks volumes. But if, as a parent, you're aware of this tendency, you can confront and deal with it when your child is still young.

A child with a Scorpio rising may be seen by others as mysterious, enigmatic and all those adjectives so frequently assigned to Scorpio, but in actuality it's a mask he wears, an image he projects. It's his persona. On the playground or in a group, these kids can be dictatorial and downright bossy, like little mafia dons. But once you call them on that behavior, once their cover is blown, they usually back down.

These kids may be fascinated by cemeteries, ghosts, UFOs or anything that goes bump in the night. And they are fearless in their pursuit of uncovering the bottom line about such phenomena.

Scorpio Children Born on the Cusp

One night at a dinner party, I met a 19-year-old woman who insisted she was a Libra. But everything about her—the way she moved and talked, the questions she asked and didn't ask—suggested that she was a Scorpio.

Later that evening, I did tarot readings for some of the people at the party, including this young woman. But when the cards were laid out, I just sat there and stared at them, unable to connect any of the dots. I felt completely blocked. I kept trying to fit the cards together into a story, but it was like trying to read Chinese. She glanced up with a rather gleeful expression on her face and said, "I'm hard to read for, aren't I?"

"You definitely are."

"It's because my life is perfect." She then proceeded to explain the ways in which her life was perfect, all the things I would expect to hear from someone who is fiercely private. I eventually got her birth information from her mother and did her chart. She was a Scorpio, right on the cusp between Libra and Scorpio.

If your child is born on the cusp between Libra and Scorpio or between Scorpio and Sagittarius, then he may exhibit traits of both signs. On the Libra side, this could include:

- Giving in too easily to other people's demands
- Dislike of confrontation
- Need for balance and harmony in life
- Deep aesthetic sense
- Sociability—much more so than a typical Scorpio
- Inability to hurt anyone's feelings
- Love of music and may have musical or artistic talent
- Trouble making time for himself because he usually tends to others' needs first
- Indecisiveness

If your child was born on the cusp between Scorpio and Sagittarius, he may exhibit some of Sadge's traits:

- Restlessness—a need to be constantly moving, doing
- Search for the big picture, not too interested in details
- Expansive thought and action
- Lust for travel
- An unquenchable thirst for experience
- Boastfulness
- Lack of secrecy
- Pursuit of the truth
- Creative drive often starts with a question: What if…?

From the Mother of a Scorpio Daughter

Julie Scully is a TV writer and the mother of five daughters. Her second oldest daughter, twenty-five-year-old Erin, is a Scorpio. I sent Julie the introduction to this chapter and asked her if it fit Erin. Here's her reply:

Erin's birth was weird. I drove an hour to the doctor because I was having contractions every minute. He said I hadn't dilated enough and sent me home. I wasn't home long when I decided to return. They gave me a shot of Demerol, and within ten minutes I was giving birth.

Erin was both a loner at times, playing off by herself, and could be the center of the party, if she chose to be so. She was and still is fiercely loyal. She's devastated when a close friend isn't as loyal.

She's very emotional and loves to discuss her feelings. She also encourages other people to be passionate and open about their feelings. It can feel like a tsunami at times.

Her edge is about half an inch deep. She has a lot of outbursts, but you're right, they're not tantrums.

I always knew Erin would do something in art since she was a tiny child. She was just so observant. Sometimes it could cause embarrassment. For instance, if I saw someone without a leg, or some other outstanding deformity or difference coming towards us, I would try and divert her attention to something else so she wouldn't see it because if she did, she'd flat out ask, "Hey, where'd your leg go?" She was direct, but not disrespectful. She truly wanted to know what happened. Most people were very tolerant of her behavior, and I'm grateful for that.

She was born with a stroke, which we didn't discover until the invention of the MRI. She was probably two to three when the machine came to L.A., back in the day when hospitals didn't have one, and the machine would travel from city to city. She would have crying jags around 4:00 to 5:00 p.m. everyday when she was a baby, and the only thing that soothed her was me singing. I think I sang

Itsy Bitsy Spider, because that was the one song that soothed her until she was in grade school. I sang to her every night before bed, and I always put music on for her at night. Growing up, Erin always had to have a few hours alone in her room listening to music.

I remember taking her to Sydney, Australia, and we'd still have to observe that routine for her. It's been only in recent years that neuroscience discovered that the part of the brain for speech is different than for singing. So some stroke patients can sing, even if they can't talk. Erin's speech was affected by the stroke, and she had difficulty retrieving words if someone asked her a direct question like, "How old are you?" She knew and would struggle to reply, "four." It was horribly frustrating for her, and sometimes she would cry.

One day I heard her playing hide-and-go-seek, and she was sing-songing the "one-two-three-four … Ready or not, here I come," announcement while covering her eyes, and she didn't miss a beat. So that's when I started teaching her spelling words, etc. by making up songs. Years later when I watched a news documentary on strokes and found out that different parts of the brain were used for speaking or singing, it all made perfect sense.

Erin breathes music. She picked up a paintbrush a few years ago, turned on the music and never stopped. With no formal training, her art is consistently breathtaking in its use of color. She captures something that our brain craves because it's so pleasing to look at them.

Oh! And she was stung by a scorpion once! She was little and always afraid of dying, so I told her it was a doodlebug so she wouldn't worry. I made up some song and kept her occupied while I captured the scorpion to show an expert in case it was the poisonous kind. It wasn't. But how many Scorpios have been stung by a scorpion? I've never been stung by a scorpion, and I grew up in the desert.

Chapter 6:

The One in Charge: The Scorpio Boss

"Speak softly—but carry a big stick."
Teddy Roosevelt, October 27

You've probably heard stories and rumors about Scorpio bosses—that they're petty tyrants and dictators who breathe down your neck, that they demand and expect too much and are way too exacting. And while there may well be Scorpio bosses who exhibit these characteristics, a boss who acts like this constantly won't remain a boss for long, and his employees will revolt or quit.

So what can you realistically expect from a Scorpio boss? First off, it depends on your boss's gender.

The dark side of the female Scorpio boss is Demi Moore in the movie version of the Michael Crichton novel *Disclosure*. Interestingly, Moore and Crichton are/were Scorpios and the theme—a female boss who uses sex to get what she wants—is definitely Scorpionic. So if you want to see a visual depiction of the dark side of the Scorpio boss, watch this film. It portrays the kind of tension and conflict inherent in this kind of situation. It's the kind of theme that makes for great storytelling, but certainly isn't the kind of dynamic you want to experience with a boss.

Your female Scorpio boss probably isn't the chatty type who asks how your kids are or how your vacation went, although she may be more prone to do that than her male counterpart. She has a clear vision about her purview as a boss and your role as an employee, and it all begins with the high standards she sets for herself. She doesn't expect more of you as an employee than she does of herself.

She doesn't hesitate to meet a challenge or to take calculated risks. Her courage and tenacity are legendary. But she is also cautious and often secretive about what she's doing, and you'll hear about it only after she has succeeded.

Her powers of perception are so strong that she can probably just take a look at you on any given day and understand your mood and state of mind. It can be a bit unsettling when she makes a remark that addresses what you're thinking. Her possessiveness about her company and her employees can be seen if and when you fraternize with the competition. Be careful! You don't want to experience her biting sarcasm or that Scorpionic sting.

The standards of a male Scorpio boss are just as high and exacting as his female counterpart, and he expects you and his other employees to meet them. He doesn't encounter too many problems in this regard because during the job interview process, he knew in less than sixty seconds if you were suited for his company. It's that power of perception again.

Your male Scorpio boss runs a tight ship, but not so tight that he's on you every second. He knows that you're a professional (and a responsible adult!) and treats you as such. You know what your job is in his hierarchy. It's not as if you're working for a boss whose goals are vague, whose plans for his company are made on the fly. This man's vision for his company is crystalline, and he has created a strategy for achieving what he foresees.

There are undoubtedly things about your Scorpio boss that puzzle or bewilder you, but just remember that his decisions often are based on his considerable intuition, his gut feeling about a product or service. So even if you don't understand his decisions, he does. And when, down the line, the company's profits triple, and as a result you get a raise, you'll realize you don't need to know why. Enjoy the ride!

Aries & the Scorpio Boss

Entrepreneurial

You were hired because of your enthusiasm, energy and incredible vivacity. You're a self-starter, a generator of ideas whose fearlessness fits well into the Scorpio scheme of things. Now let's take a closer look at how to maintain a harmonious relationship with your Scorpio boss so that both you and the company succeed!

Using Your Strengths

Your mission, Aries, should you choose to accept it, is to find new ways and to try new methods that enable Scorpio's company or services to expand and grow. Live the *Star Trek* motto that fits your sign—go where no man (or woman) has gone before. Look for gaps in the market that the company might fill. Be the intrepid explorer you are and follow your passions.

Generate as many ideas as you want and make your case for each of them. Some won't pan out, but for the ones that do, make sure you have a plan that explains how the idea can be implemented. Don't fly by the seat of your pants. Once an idea has met Scorpio's approval, get out of the way and let another employee—perhaps an earth sign?—carry things through.

Stand Up for What You Believe

If you're passionate about one of the ideas you've generated and that Scorpio has nixed, don't give up. It means you haven't presented the case in a way that adequately expresses your passion and why you think the idea would work.

First, go back to the drawing board. Do more research. Don't hesitate to enlist the help of co-workers who are as enthusiastic about the idea as you are. A Virgo can help you to connect the dots and dive into the details. A Taurus co-worker will persist until the strategy is laid out. A Gemini will spread the word about your concept. You get the idea. Draw on the strengths and abilities of your co-workers.

When you're ready to present your idea again, when you're standing up for what you believe in, let your passion shine! Scorpio may then see things differently.

It's unlikely that a Scorpio boss will ever ask you to do something that's against your principles. But if your boss is the Demi Moore type in *Disclosure*, there may be a situation where that happens. I recently heard a rather harrowing story about a Scorpio female boss whose company provides an entertainment service to downtown bars and restaurants. She hires outside contractors to carry out these services, and they are assigned to particular venues on particular dates. One of these outside contractors had told her weeks in advance that he wouldn't be able to make one of his assignments due to a prior commitment. The Scorpio boss forgot about it and didn't get anyone else to cover for the man. The restaurant owner was angry about it, and the Scorpio boss blamed the outside contractor.

During the contractor's yearly review, Scorpio informed him that he wasn't getting a raise because of what had happened. He showed her the text message he'd sent her about not being able to make it on that particular date and her response that she would get someone to cover for him. It was clearly her fault, not his. But instead of apologizing, she asked him to lie to the restaurant owner, to say he was at fault. He refused—and is now looking for another job.

Set Goals

Life is often so immediate for you that it's a challenge for you to think ahead, to set goals. But with a Scorpio boss, one of your prime directives is to set goals. Have a list of daily, weekly and monthly goals. Keep the list on your phone, your iPad, your computer or wherever it's most accessible. At the end of each day, week or month, check your list to see what you've achieved.

Once you get into the habit of doing this, it could become second nature to you, Aries, and you won't need the written list anymore. If you're out to impress your Scorpio boss, this is one sure way of doing it—as long as you actually follow through on achieving the goals!

Compatibility

Let's get the bad news out of the way first: you and Scorpio aren't the most compatible of signs. In fact, you're probably better suited for self-employment, Aries, where you're the one calling the shots and making the decisions. However, this relationship can be mutually beneficial if Scorpio can overlook your tendency to be argumentative and if you can overlook your boss's tendency to see everything as black or white, either/or.

The ideal situation for this boss/employee relationship consists of small, but significant, details that collectively strengthen the relationship:

For Scorpio:

➢ Give Aries a lot of freedom in her job. She'll be happier and will produce more, and what she contributes will increase your bottom line.
➢ Build flexibility into Aries's schedule. Let her work from home sometimes.
➢ Capitalize on her ability to generate ideas and on her people skills. She excels at networking and will bring in more customers and clients.
➢ Don't impose restrictions on her.

For Aries:

- ➤ Finish what you start.
- ➤ Do what you say you'll do.
- ➤ Build alliances.
- ➤ Tackle every task you're assigned, even the ones that may not interest you all that much, with your abundant energy and passion.

Keeping Scorpio Happy

Your boss is happiest when the company's reputation and visibility are rising, profits are increasing and everything is humming along as it should be. Do your part to make that happen, and you'll land a raise and a promotion.

You & Your Muse

In order for you to bring maximum creativity to your job, be sure your muse is primed and ready all the time. An impulse is often the most direct communication from your muse and the easiest to act on. Follow such impulses to wherever they lead you. Chances are that your muse has a clearer idea about what's going on than you do!

Taurus & the Scorpio Boss

Tenacity

It's likely that you were hired because Scorpio felt the chemistry was right. Perhaps you felt the same thing during your initial interview, and no wonder. In the astrological scheme of things, you two are polar opposites who create a powerful balance for each other. Your respective elements, earth and water, get along just fine, and you're both fixed signs. You're also equally stubborn, which can be a problem, but we'll explore that more in the compatibility section. Let's see how this relationship works on a daily basis.

Using Your Strengths

Your tenacity and resilience match that of Scorpio. Once you start something—whether it's reading a book or climbing Everest—you usually finish it. As far as your Scorpio boss is concerned, your persistence and tenacity are your greatest strengths. You also have deep reservoirs of creative energy and a knack for making the abstract so practical that anyone can understand it and use it.

You aren't the type who likes sitting at a desk all day long. It goes against your grain. Besides, some of your best creative ideas come to you when you're involved in physical activity. If you can break up your workday with a brisk walk or a yoga class, you'll be far more productive. Your Scorpio boss may go for the idea and even join you!

One of the interesting dynamics between you and your Scorpio boss is that he may see strengths in you that you don't even know you have. The reverse is also true.

Stand Up for What You Believe

You won't have any problem doing this. As fixed signs, both you and Scorpio have firm ideas about what's right and what's wrong and what's beneficial or not for the company or the service you provide.

If there's something about your job that you would like to be doing differently, then write out your approach and explain why you believe it will work. Back it with facts. Or, if you have a strong intuitive sense about this approach—or have received information through dreams and synchronicities—lay that out, too. Scorpio will listen closely.

Taurus can be as intuitive as Scorpio but often demands proof that the intuition is correct. So when you provide Scorpio with your intuitive impressions about something, it's only after you have scrutinized and rigorously cross-examined it.

Set Goals

Some people drift from one task to another in their jobs, without any particular goal in mind. They're just putting in their time. But for you, that's like embarking across a vast ocean without a rudder or direction. You need more than a series of tasks strung together from one day to the next. You need to know not only where you're going but also how you'll get there. And what better way to do that than setting goals? It's something that comes naturally to you.

Whether you set goals daily, weekly, monthly or even annually, it's important to write them down. That makes them more concrete, real and tangible, and it's easier to gauge your progress. If you're in sales, you might keep daily goals about how many products you would like to sell or aim for a specific dollar amount.

You can be sure that your Scorpio boss has her own list of goals for the company—the day-to-day minutiae as well as goals for the larger picture.

Compatibility

This employee/boss relationship is generally compatible, and it's about balancing each other's strengths and weaknesses. The major challenge in this combination is that you're equally stubborn individuals who don't compromise unless you're convinced the other person's way is the right way.

Since you're the employee and not the boss, Taurus, this could be a problem for you. However, if you and Scorpio have a solid working relationship, and she encourages her employees to offer their opinions, then speak up and be heard!

Here are some other tips for both you and Scorpio for keeping this working relationship on an even keel.

For Scorpio:

> ➤ It's not necessary to keep close tabs on Taurus or to try to control what he does and when he does it. Like his fellow earth signs Capricorn and Virgo, he's industrious and disciplined.

> ➤ Taurus moves at his own pace. If you urge him to move faster, it's likely he'll dig in his heels and refuse to budge at all.

> ➤ If you and Taurus disagree on a principle, hear him out. Don't just cut him off because you're so certain your way is the only way.

For Taurus:

> ➤ If you're annoyed or angered by something your Scorpio boss does or says, keep it to yourself until you're calmer. Then express it in an email or in person.

> ➤ You can be as secretive as Scorpio; so don't hold that against him! But if you really need to know what's going on, particularly if it concerns you, then ask.

> ➤ When in doubt about Scorpio's motives, give him the benefit of the doubt.

Keeping Scorpio Happy

Granted, it's not your job to make Scorpio happy or to keep her happy. But if you enjoy your job, there are certain things you can do to make sure you're not the one whose position is cut in the event of downsizing.

> ➤ Make yourself indispensable—but not at a cost to anyone else.

> ➤ Carry through on anything you promise. You tend to do this anyway, but in an employee/boss relationship, it's important.

You & Your Muse

In order for you to bring maximum creativity to your job, your muse must be nurtured and tended to, and when she speaks you have to be ready to act. The Taurus muse often speaks to you through synchronicities, so don't dismiss a coincidence as meaningless, as random. If the significance isn't immediately obvious, dig a little deeper. Try to understand the symbols. Request a dream that will explain it.

Gemini & the Scorpio Boss

Networking

Hey, Gemini! Have you or your twin ever wondered why Scorpio hired you? Of course you have. Within just a few minutes, he recognized that your gift of gab could be a valuable asset to his company. He liked your vibrant energy, wit and the way you think quickly on your feet. While this employee/boss combination may not be the most compatible or harmonious, it's certainly never boring. You keep Scorpio amused and bewildered, and he prompts you to dig beneath the surface. How's this work on a daily basis?

Using Your Strengths

You're a consummate communicator with a large network of friends and acquaintances. You're also an information junkie, and when you don't know the answer to something, you usually know where to go or who to ask for the answer. You are bored to death in a desk job, and if Scorpio is smart, she'll put you out in front of the pubic to do what you do best.

If you're one of those Geminis who have twice the energy of the people around you, then you're able to accomplish quite a bit in a given day as long as you aren't distracted. Scorpio probably realizes this about you and utilizes it to the company's advantage.

Stand Up for What You Believe

Even when you're irked or dissatisfied by a policy or task that Scorpio has implemented, some part of you understands why your boss made the decision he did. Blame it on the duality inherent in your sign. What angers one twin is shrugged off by the other twin, unless the issue involves something about which you're passionate. Then the fury of both twins comes into play.

A Gemini friend of mine worked for a year in a large city library. Her boss was a female Scorpio. Every afternoon, the boss would call her employees into her office and read something out of the Bible to them. My Gemini friend found the practice offensive and told her boss that she didn't feel religious preaching belonged in a professional setting. This was a city library, not a church or religious organization. Scorpio shrugged off her objections and said that attendance was mandatory.

To get around it, this Gemini started making herself scarce around three every afternoon. She found stuff to do in other departments. When her boss called her on it, she bluntly told her she refused to attend these little afternoon sessions. She desperately wanted to quit, but couldn't afford to, even though all the signs indicated she should. Not long afterward, she was fired. It was, she said later, the best thing that ever happened to her.

When you stand up for what you believe, understand that there may be consequences!

Set Goals

If you begin each week with a list of goals, it will keep you focused, provide you with a definite direction and ultimately will save you time. Make the goals specific. Instead of saying that you're going to pick up new clients this week, choose a realistic number—five or ten—and then spell out how you're going to find these new clients.

Perhaps you attend workshops or conventions related to your profession or you pick up new clients through referrals from your network of friends and acquaintances. If your company is active on social media, maybe you do it that way. Select several venues for the week. Be detailed, but not so detailed that you box yourself in.

Compatibility

Typically, air and water signs aren't terribly compatible. But because you're a chameleon who can fit in virtually anywhere, compatibility probably won't be an issue unless Scorpio pushes one of your buttons, as in the example of the Gemini woman who worked in a city library. To keep this employee/boss relationship humming along without drama, here are some tips for both you and Scorpio.

For Scorpio:

➤ The best way to utilize Gemini's talents is to put him in charge of communication or public relations for your company. Or put him in charge of the company's social media platforms.

➤ Give him ample freedom to do his job. Flexible hours or even working from home a couple days a week would suit him.

➤ Keep his brain even busier than it is by tapping him for creative brainstorming sessions.

For Gemini:

➤ As a mutable sign, you may be the one to surrender in a disagreement. Weigh your options carefully and decide if the disagreement is worth winning. If it is, then don't be a pushover.

➤ Don't ever stretch the truth. Scorpio's perspicacity will detect it.

➤ When you want something from your boss, don't talk circles around him. Be direct and forthright.

Keeping Scorpio Happy

Go for the bottom line: help to increase the company's reputation, visibility and profit.

You & Your Muse

In order for you to bring maximum creativity to your job you should listen to your muse when she speaks. The Gemini muse often appears in one of those peak, *Aha!* moments when something snaps into perfect clarity for you. That's the Gemini muse screaming at the top of her lungs to be heard, dancing in wild circles in celebration of the marriage of left and right brain.

Cancer & the Scorpio Boss

Effortless

During your interview with Scorpio, something clicked between the two of you, a certain innate understanding of how the other sees the world. Scorpio glimpsed your expansive imagination and your ability to nurture creativity in self and others. You recognized Scorpio's persistence and her vision for the company. When you were hired, the company became your new home. Here, you knew you could use your talents and abilities to help create something special.

Using Your Strengths

When you're immersed in a project, your laser-like focus matches Scorpio's. You can intuitively envision the final product and feel your way from one point to the next with the tenacity of the crab that symbolizes your sign. You're able to sense alternate paths you might take, and if and when you follow one of them, it's because your emotional and intuitive feelers signal that you should.

Your introspection, your constant vigilance of your creative inner process is so finely tuned that you rarely falter once you've embarked on a project, goal or mission. But when you do, giving up isn't an option. You simply find another way of getting to where you want to be. As a moon-ruled cardinal sign, your extraordinary memory is intimately tied to your deepest emotions. A familiar scent or taste can trigger the origin of a particular memory, and it's just as bright and clear in your head as the day it happened. For Scorpio, this kind of extraordinary memory is a major plus, and you can be sure your boss will tap it from time to time.

Stand Up for What You Believe

Many Cancers go to great lengths to avoid emotional confrontation. If you're that type, then when you stand up for yourself you do so by being evasive, coy or perhaps even subversive.

Let's say, for instance, that you work in an advertising company—think *Mad Men*, but set in the present. Your Scorpio boss assigns you an account for a product or for a company to which you have a moral objection. Maybe you're a pacifist and the company manufactures military weapons. But because this account is the largest the agency has ever landed, you're certain your objection won't matter.

Instead of asking Scorpio to assign the account to someone else, you decide to create an ad campaign against war and the invasion of sovereign countries. When you present the campaign to your boss and co-workers, a stunned silence grips the room. You've made your objection clear and now comes the moment of reckoning.

How will your Scorpio boss react? Will you be fired? Will the campaign be assigned to one of your co-workers? However it pans out, you're prepared. Standing up for what you believe always involves risk.

Set Goals

Your emotions are your most powerful resource, but because of your acute sensitivity, it's easy for you to get stuck in negative emotions. So the goals you set should be internal and personal, focused only on positive energy and emotion. By allowing yourself to be a vehicle for optimism and upbeat emotions and thoughts, you're better prepared to carry out your professional responsibilities and are able to work at maximum creative capacity.

Since your Scorpio boss has to do this to some extent as well, it could lead to an innovative practice in the company—perhaps a meditation or gentle yoga class before the workday begins?

Compatibility

As a pair of water signs, you and your boss should be extremely compatible. There may be times, though, when you feel overwhelmed by Scorpio's intensity, and then you scuttle off into a corner or take a sick day. To keep this employee/boss relationship moving in the right direction, here are some tips for both of you.

For Scorpio:

➢ Cancer needs physical and emotional space in order to perform well on the job. Her office should be hers alone, to arrange and decorate however she wants. It will provide her with her home away from home, give her a greater sense of security and will keep her creative energy high.

➢ If she can work from home periodically, she'll be happier and more productive.

For Cancer:

➢ Try not to take everything Scorpio says and does personally. It's a waste of energy and, besides, it probably isn't about you, anyway.

➢ Learn to vocalize what you're feeling, when you're feeling it. Don't keep stuff bottled up inside.

➢ Always take a few minutes to ground yourself creatively before you dive into your work for the day.

Keeping Scorpio Happy

Stay in your creative groove. Produce, produce and be happy!

You & Your Muse

In order for you to bring maximum creativity to your job, it's vital to listen to your muse when she speaks, and she often does so through symbols. Since symbols are the stuff of your inner world, you recognize them as messages from your unconscious and instinctively understand how to decipher them. Some of these symbols may be nudging you toward taking a creative risk. You may initially resist the risk, but remember that any risk involves faith that you're taking the right path.

Leo & the Scorpio Boss

Vibrant

During your interview, Scorpio wasn't fooled by your act, Leo. He knew you were *on* and that he was your audience. He was impressed with your vivaciousness, buoyant personality, passion and obvious talent. He was also surprised and delighted that you already had a million ideas about how you could help the company expand not only nationally, but also internationally. He liked that you *think big*. So he hired you on the spot.

Now, Leo, can you live up to the promise of your sign?

Using Your Strengths

Flair. Generosity. Courage. Creativity. Tenacity. Those words are some that are used to describe your personality. All are true, and some are truer than others. Figure out how you can draw on all your personal resources with this job, this career path, and then charge ahead. Your muse is primed and ready!

Maybe you're the costume designer for a small theater company that Scorpio started several years ago. You've got six months to prepare four costumes for the next play. What happens for you creatively between now and then? Your passion and excitement ratchet upward, and you throw yourself into your work with twelve-hour days, endless sketches, bolts of fabric and patterns. Your muse is so caught up in the work that the weeks and months fly by. And in the end, your tenacity pays off big time. The costumes—and the play—are a huge success.

When you're engaged creatively, the process *is* the flair, *is* the drama. And Scorpio and your audience are applauding.

Stand Up for What You Believe

As a fixed fire sign, you probably don't have any problem standing up for what you believe. But if you're standing up to a Scorpio boss with a piercing gaze that seems to peer down inside your soul, your thoughts immediately zips to possible unemployment. You play a mind game with yourself:

If I tell him no, he might fire me.
If I tell him no and explain why, he might still fire me.
If I lose my job, I'll be broke in a month. Forget it. Not worth it.

Then you toss and turn most of the night, berating yourself for your cowardice and your lack of backbone, knowing you'll be miserable if you have to do whatever this is about. But because you're as stubborn as Scorpio and feel so strongly about this, you go into work the next morning and ask your boss if you can speak to him privately.

You lay out your objections and/or beliefs about this and do it with all your usual passion and flair and are so convincing that Scorpio replies, "Let me think about it."

Whether you win or not is irrelevant. The point is that you stood up for what you believed.

Set Goals

Since Leos often suffer great insecurities—which is why you (ego) so often crave an audience and applause—your first and primary goal is to love and approve of yourself so that other people's opinions cease to matter. "No matter what the problem, the main issue to work on is LOVNG THE SELF," wrote medical intuitive and author Louise Hay. "This is the 'magic wand' that dissolves problems. Part of self-acceptance is releasing other people's opinions."

If you can achieve this, Leo, then everything else—including the professional goals you set—will take care of itself.

Compatibility

On the surface, Leo and Scorpio aren't particularly compatible. However, because you're both fixed signs, you understand each other's tenacity and persistence and are able to capitalize on those qualities. Conflict may surface as a result of other traits you and Scorpio share—stubbornness and a reluctance to change your opinions and beliefs. To keep this employee/boss relationship harmonious, here are some tips for both of you:

For Scorpio:

➤ Give Leo breathing space to do her thing. Once she's fully engaged in a project, she works tirelessly to produce what she's promised.

➤ In a standoff, listen to her objections, ideas and concerns. Consider them rather than dismissing them outright.

➤ Allow her flexibility in her schedule. If she puts in a couple of twelve-hour days, tell her to take Friday off so she can enjoy a long weekend. You get the idea, Scorpio. Give her every reason to stay!

For Leo:

➤ Try not to take everything personally. Granted, this may be a challenge for you. But by letting other people's remarks or actions just roll away from you, you'll find that your physical, emotional and spiritual energy increase.

➤ Take a few minutes each morning to put yourself in a positive frame of mind. Surround yourself with positive energy. It then becomes your shield and your ally.

➤ Love what you do—and the applause will follow.

Keeping Scorpio Happy

Here are some simple, common-sense guidelines to keeping Scorpio happy:

➤ Follow through on what you say you'll do.

➤ Be honest, forthright and direct.

➤ Remain true to the vision Scorpio has for the company.

You & Your Muse

In order for you to bring maximum creativity to your job, your connection to your muse should be unfettered so you hear her (or him) without distractions. Your muse loves to play, to have fun and speaks to you most clearly when you engage in an activity that you're doing strictly for enjoyment. Each day, do something just for the pleasure of it, and don't be surprised when you're flooded with ideas.

Virgo & the Scorpio Boss

Agility

During your interview, Scorpio was impressed by your presence—your mental quickness, the way you spoke, your curiosity, your easy laughter and your personality. You, in turn, felt comfortable talking with Scorpio about her vision for her company and what your job would entail. The effortless flow between the two of you may have extended the interview and at the end of it, you got the job.

Now what, Virgo?

Using Your Strengths

Your steel-trap mind churns through endless bits of data, collating details and sculpting them according to some inner blueprint of perfection. It's irrelevant whether the rest of us have any idea what you're doing. *You* know, and that's all that matters.

You and Gemini share a common ruler, Mercury, but your approaches to life are different. Where Gemini collects information and communicates it, you collect information, sift through it all for the details that matter and attempt to make it all practical. Along the way, you are precisely discriminating with the information you collect. Whatever you deem to be extraneous is tossed out. Your ideal of perfection is never compromised. This gift is what you bring to the table.

Stand Up for What You Believe

As a mutable earth sign, you are more likely to avoid confrontation than Scorpio is. But sometimes, standing up for what you believe means standing up for yourself, and you aren't as likely to back down even when you're up against Scorpio.

You may not react immediately—unless you have a heavy Leo influence in your chart. You'll mull things over, pick it all apart, dissect it and then you'll piece it all back together again, but in a new way. And when you're sure of what you want to say, certain that your point of view is right on target, you'll make your case to Scorpio. Thanks to your calm, collected way of presenting everything, Scorpio comes around to your way of thinking.

Set Goals

You can set goals with startling efficiency, making endless lists of what you want to accomplish and by when. The trick, though, is to keep the goals realistic.

Perhaps you work in the entertainment industry, and one of the goals you've set is to bring in a certain number of new clients in the next month. Is the number you selected realistic? If it isn't, don't hesitate to set your sights a bit lower. It's better to do that than to become discouraged and give up altogether. Goals can always be readjusted, recalibrated.

Because you're so detailed-oriented, you may include too many details in your goals, so the universe has no wiggle room. Go general, back the goals with intense desire and act as if you've already achieved them. Then get out of your own way.

Compatibility

You and Scorpio are generally very compatible. You're both able to discern patterns, although you do it in vastly different ways. Scorpio's venue is emotions and intuition; yours is connecting a million details until the pattern—the big picture—is staring you in the face. You're both industrious individuals, hard workers who don't shy away from any task because it's too big. You may at times feel overwhelmed by your boss's intensity, and Scorpio may get frustrated with your occasional bouts of nitpickiness. But all things considered, those things are minor. Here are some tips for keeping your relationship harmonious.

For Scorpio:

➤ Take it easy with intensity stuff when you're dealing with Virgo. You don't have to be didactic or bossy with him. Once you've laid out whatever it is you want him to do, it'll get done.

➤ Listen carefully to Virgo's observations and suggestions. Her ideas are usually based on careful scrutiny.

➤ Compliment him on a job well done.

For Virgo:

➤ Take nothing personally when you're dealing with Scorpio.

➤ If you're the target of sarcasm, use wit to counteract it. Then let it all roll away.

➤ Make time for relaxation and fun.

Keeping Scorpio Happy

It's simpler than you might think: produce.

You & Your Muse

In order for you to bring maximum creativity to your job, your muse needs room to breathe. Sometimes she hollers, sometimes she whispers and sometimes she speaks to you through other means. But she speaks most clearly when you, Virgo, are *plugged in* to whatever you're doing, when you merge with whatever you're doing and the rest of the world vanishes.

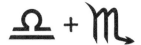

Libra & the Scorpio Boss

Balance

It didn't take long in your interview for Scorpio to make up her mind about hiring you. Your presence radiates calm (even if it's not always how you feel!), a perfect decorum, as though nothing in the world ever ruffles you. While discussing what your job position would entail, you stepped into Scorpio's shoes and saw it from his point of view. Even though your view differed, both views were right. You can live with that paradox. It's your gift.

Using Your Strengths

When you're surrounded by people who can't agree, you enter your element. You begin to mediate the disagreements—quietly, unobtrusively and gradually, harmony and peace reign again. This is the Libra magic at work. Your people skills are finely honed, and Scorpio will draw on them.

As a cardinal air sign, your ability to focus all your energy on a task or project equals or even surpasses that of Scorpio. Once you're in that flow, you're swept along with it and usually don't quit until the job is done. It can be emotionally draining for you, though, so try to pace yourself. Balance is what you're seeking, and when you're working for a Scorpio, it can be challenging to find that equilibrium.

Go ahead and take risks by doing something in a way you haven't done before. You do it in your personal life, so do it when you work for Scorpio, too. He'll admire it, and you'll be happy with the result.

Stand Up for What You Believe

Because you avoid conflict, standing up for what you believe can be difficult for you at times. You swing from peace at any cost to choosing your battles carefully. One thing is for sure, though. When you do stand up for yourself, it's utterly clear to everyone around you that you aren't the pushover you sometimes appear to be.

Let's say you're a screenwriter with a Scorpio agent. Your agent thinks you should rewrite vast sections of your screenplay. But everything inside of you screams that Scorpio is wrong. Instead of doing the rewrites, you send him an email that lays out why you wrote the screenplay the way you did; he won't relent. So you submit the screenplay to an independent producer and your relationship with your Scorpio agent ends. Drastic, perhaps, but a battle over a creative product is worth the fight.

Set Goals

For you, setting goals nearly always begins with working on yourself—finding that calm center within. That calm center is where the paradoxes you live with can't touch you, and you know it's the place from which your professional achievements unfold. A week's worth of goals might look something like this:

➢ Meditate 15 minutes daily.
➢ Take one yoga class.
➢ Walk briskly for 30 minutes three times a week.
➢ Go to the gym twice a week.
➢ Finish reading the novel I started 6 months ago.
➢ Be decisive about everything.
➢ Stay in the creative flow.

In other words, these aren't professional goals, per se, but necessary personal goals that facilitate all areas of your life.

Compatibility

You and Scorpio aren't the most compatible duo. Air and water generally aren't. But because you've mastered the art of social camouflage and avoid conflict, lack of astrological compatibility shouldn't be an issue very often, if ever. However, to keep this employee/boss relationship harmonious at all times, here are some suggestions for both of you.

For Scorpio:

➢ Tap Libra's people skills, particularly her ability to negotiate and mediate.

➢ She has a highly developed aesthetic/artistic sense. Encourage her to use it, and give her space to do so.

➢ Make sure she knows it's okay to take time for herself!

For Libra:

➢ Don't bend like a straw just to accommodate Scorpio. Establish parameters and personal space.

➢ Work independently whenever possible—from home, if you can. It will help you to remain grounded.

Keeping Scorpio Happy

By maintaining your own equilibrium, your ability to produce and create soars. The more you produce, the happier it makes Scorpio.

You & Your Muse

In order for you to bring maximum creativity to your job, it's important to listen to your muse when she speaks. Since you're such a people-oriented individual, your muse often speaks to you through friends and acquaintances. You might be thinking about taking a particular direction with a project, but are still mulling things over when someone you know mentions this very thing. Sometimes your muse speaks to you through art or music. Perhaps you're driving to work, listening to the radio and a song comes on that seems to address the issue.

Scorpio & the Scorpio Boss

Psychic

Before you interviewed with Scorpio, you probably had a hunch that you would get the job, or maybe you had a dream or a premonition about it. You've had these feelings throughout your life, and they usually turn out to be right. So during the interview, you projected complete confidence and certainty. And yes, you landed the job. But when two Scorpios work together and one of them is the boss, there are going to be power struggles.

Using Your Strengths

Your approach to work—to nearly everything in life—is to persist until you get it exactly the way you want it. Until it feels right. You don't place any time parameters on it. You simply throw yourself into the project or assignment and swim with the powerful current of your creative drive.

Water signs tend to be introspective, but for you that introspection can be utterly ruthless and relentless. Even when you're engaged in something mundane—like walking to the water fountain outside your office—a part of you is analyzing how you feel about what you're doing. You're picking things apart, looking for that absolute bottom line. Your boss, of course, understands this aspect of your personality because he's the same way. If he's smart, he'll leave you alone and let the process unfold.

Stand Up for What You Believe

You do this constantly; it's second nature to you. You do it through the choices you make as a consumer, at the voting booth, with the people you choose as friends and with the schools your kids attend. But with your work, there are definite hot spots that elicit a strong and often immediate reaction:

- Criticism you believe is unfair and unjust.
- When the work you've done is attributed to someone else.
- When you're told your way is the wrong way and you know otherwise.
- Being ignored or dismissed as irrelevant.

You probably won't make a scene. Flagrant drama in a confrontation is a waste of time and energy. You're more likely to compose a carefully worded email to your boss, detailing why you disagree and citing facts and statistics that back up your viewpoint. Even if you don't get what you want or deserve, you never back down.

Set Goals

You probably set goals frequently. Maybe you even keep actual lists of what you would like to achieve daily, weekly, monthly or annually. You dislike wasting time, and setting goals provides you with a definite direction, a way forward.

Your goals usually aren't so detailed that you stifle the creative process, an important factor in your relationship with your muse. She often has her own agenda and sometimes that agenda is to make you work for what you want or need. This is when synchronicity can come into play, where a string of meaningful coincidences nudge you in a particular direction or enable you to find what you need when you need it.

Compatibility

Yes, you and your Scorpio boss are so compatible that you often read each other's minds. You pick up on each other's moods and concerns to the point where you sometimes have to shut down the intuitive side of your brain.

The big challenge in your working for a Scorpio is the power issue. Who's the boss and who's the employee? Your Scorpio boss may be confronting the same issue from time to time, so the two of you may have to sit down and actually discuss it! Here are some tips for both of you to make sure your relationship remains harmonious.

For the Scorpio Boss:
➢ Don't make assumptions. Just because your employee is also a Scorpio, it doesn't mean you understand her completely and can anticipate what she'll do. As you well know, Scorpios are an enigma even to themselves!

➢ Give her the emotional space and time she needs to fulfill her responsibilities.

➢ In a disagreement, give her the same consideration that you would like to be given.

For the Scorpio Employee:
➢ Read that first bulleted point for the Scorpio boss. This also applies to you.

➢ Take nothing for granted. Just because you and your boss often have this telepathic connection, it's smart to clarify through verbal communication.

➢ Relax. Trust that it's all going to work out.

Keeping Scorpio Happy
Look in the mirror. What makes you happy? What *keeps* you happy? Define it and carry it out. It's really as simple as that.

You & Your Muse
In order for you to bring your maximum creativity to the job, listen to your muse! She (or he) speaks most clearly when you take outings to get your creative flow moving. A park. A museum. A concert. A long walk. Your senses are stimulated, and suddenly, things begin to click in your head, and ideas race through you.

Sagittarius & the Scorpio Boss

Expansion

Ah, you can be quite the charmer—vivacious, outspoken and funny. But during your interview, Scorpio saw through your charm and recognized something you two have in common. You're both in pursuit of the truth. You're constantly on the lookout for the big picture, and Scorpio is searching for the absolute bottom line. Your approaches to this pursuit differ, but eventually get you to the same place.

So how does all this work out on a daily basis? Let's take a closer look.

Using Your Strengths

Thanks to Jupiter, the planet that rules your sign, your talents are diverse and rarely confined to just one area or interest. One of the most famous Sadges, Nostradamus, wasn't just a seer/prophet. He was also a physician and an astrologer with knowledge of alchemy and magic. No matter what you take on or what you tackle, your various creative talents come into play. It's all part of the way you sift through information. Even when you can't connect the dots that lead to the big picture you're seeking, you're capable of grasping the tangents.

Scorpio understands this about you, and if he doesn't, it won't take him long to figure it out. He'll tap your diverse talents and make sure your responsibilities are flexible and expansive enough so you don't get bored.

Stand Up for What You Believe

You never have a problem standing up for what you believe. In fact, some Sagittarians do this so frequently they can be downright obnoxious about it. The trick for you is to choose your battles carefully—like when a principle is involved. With your work, there are definite situations and issues that will elicit an immediate response from you.

> ➢ The stifling of your creative freedom
> ➢ Having to punch a clock
> ➢ A boss who throws his weight around just because he can
> ➢ An unappreciative boss

In any of these situations, you probably won't hold back in your objections. They'll be immediate and blunt.

Set Goals

Sadges are sometimes depicted as individuals who are too busy traveling and *doing stuff* to set goals. But what these descriptions don't say is that you're capable of setting goals regardless of where you are or what you're doing. You don't necessarily need a list or a computer file. Your goals are tucked away in one compartment of your busy mind, and you check them when you need to.

Typically, your work goals involve some larger search or quest. Perhaps you're in law school and are interning at the law firm where Scorpio is your boss. In your free time, you're also writing a legal thriller. So perhaps one of your daily goals is to combine research for your boss that expands your knowledge of a particular area in your novel.

Compatibility

Now we're down to the nitty gritty. Generally speaking, you and Scorpio aren't known for your compatibility. You're a mutable fire sign, and Scorpio is a fixed water sign. However, you each have traits the other admires and strengths the other doesn't, so your working relationship must be a give-and-take. Here are some tips for both of you on how to maintain harmony in your employee/boss relationship so that the larger entity, the company, benefits.

For Scorpio:

➤ To maximize Sagittarius's contributions to your company, give him plenty of breathing space. He knows what he's doing and understands his responsibilities.

➤ If possible, make Sadge's schedule flexible so she doesn't feel like she's punching a clock.

➤ If your company requires their employees to travel, tap Sadge. His nomadic soul will be deliriously happy.

For Sagittarius:

➤ Don't try to figure out your Scorpio boss. What's important in this relationship is that you uphold your end of the deal.

➤ If Scorpio does or says something that offends you or your principles, don't explode. Take a few deep breaths; think carefully about why you're reacting the way you are. Then discuss it with her, calmly and rationally.

➤ Find common ground, but don't always be the one who gives in during a disagreement.

Keeping Scorpio Happy

Scorpio is happiest when everyone is doing his or her job, and the company is turning a handsome profit.

You & Your Muse

Regardless of what your job entails, you attempt to be creative at it. That means you have to get in touch with your muse. But she's a tricky one and wily. She has moods, worries and issues. She has a *life*. She's every bit as independent as you are. But even when she's in the midst of her life, she doesn't forget you. Let's say you're blocked; you just can't get the creative juices flowing. Then, while running errands for your boss, a song on the radio catches your attention. *Do what you want to do…* And suddenly, creative adrenaline rushes through your veins; you're plugged in and on a roll.

Sometimes, it can be just that simple.

Capricorn & the Scorpio Boss

Worker Bees

Serious-minded, aloof, disciplined, responsible, industrious: these are the qualities Scorpio recognized in you during your interview. She liked that it was all balanced with a quick, easy laugh and decided you were the person for the job. The compatibility factor is high with this employee/boss combination, with one possible glitch: you, like Scorpio, feel the need to rule the kingdom you occupy. Power struggles could ensue. But let's see how this relationship unfolds on a daily basis.

Using Your Strengths

Others sometimes perceive you as secretive—maybe Scorpio even thinks you match him in that department! But it isn't a defensive mechanism, as it often is with Scorpio, and is due to your penchant for privacy. Within that very private world you're a builder, and nowhere is it more apparent than in your creative expression. Whether you're building a career, a garden, a fortune or a literary world, you build one step at a time and are methodical and consistent.

When you undertake a task—any task—you do so with utter commitment. Like the goat that symbolizes your sign, you keep climbing until you reach the summit, achieve the goal and finish the project. So don't be surprised when Scorpio assigns you with difficult tasks and challenging projects. He knows you're the one that will get the job done!

Stand Up for What You Believe

Never let it be said that you back down from a fight when your principles are involved or when you are unjustly criticized about the work you've done. Then you become the goat on the hillside that battles any invading creature, even if that creature is larger and fiercer.

As a cardinal earth sign, you move in a singular direction, focused not only on the goal, but the process. Although it's unlikely that Scorpio will get in your way, you don't hesitate to stand up to her if she does. There won't be any drama, just a tough as nails, straightforward response where you lay out your complaints, observations and suggestions. It's difficult, even for a Scorpio, to dismiss what you say.

Set Goals

You Capricorns are masters at setting and achieving goals. If there's any point where you doubt your ability to do this, then set small goals for yourself, bite-sized daily or weekly goals. Once you realize how easy it is for you to reach these smaller goals, the big ones won't be a problem.

When goals are born from an intense desire, you have the uncanny ability to find what you need when you need it, and to manifest opportunities that help you to achieve that goal. With focus and crystallized ambition, you raise this ability to an art form.

Since your sign is ruled by Saturn, you feel comfortable with structured goals within a structured environment. Scorpio sensed that about you in the initial interview and capitalizes on its daily.

Compatibility

Earth and water are usually so compatible that your working relationship with Scorpio should hum along on an even keel. If and when it doesn't, it's probably due to an external factor rather than to a clash of personalities. But here are some tips for both of you to maintain a strong and harmonious relationship.

For Scorpio:

➤ You know his strengths and skills and don't hesitate to capitalize on them. But don't ever take him for granted. Like you, he rarely forgets a slight, and the bigger the slight, the more difficult it is for him to forgive.

➤ Within the structure of her responsibilities, be sure to build in personal time so she can recharge. This time is so integral to her creative health that if she ignores it, she's inviting problems and complications. She won't take time for herself unless it's built into the job!

➤ Express appreciation for her work.

For Capricorn:

➤ In a disagreement, don't just sit there and fume. Express what you feel and why.

➤ As the workaholic of the zodiac, it's vital to carve out time for yourself. Hit the gym, go hiking, take a yoga or Pilates class or do whatever it is you enjoy.

➤ When you're stuck creatively, mine your dreams. Keep a notepad next to your bed, and before you fall asleep, request a dream that will give you whatever you need.

Keeping Scorpio Happy

When you're happy, you're more productive. And that keeps Scorpio happy.

You & Your Muse

As a cardinal sign, you may hear your muse speak most clearly through impulses, which are signals to do something differently than you usually do. When you follow an impulse, you're answering a summons from your soul, your higher self or whatever name you want to give it. An impulse is an invitation to plug into your creativity and to be daring and adventurous.

Aquarius & the Scorpio Boss

Unconventional

During your interview with Scorpio, he sensed that you are a paradigm buster, someone who definitely thinks outside the box, and knew your skills would be a valuable asset for his company. For you, though, busting a paradigm is simply empty rebellion unless something larger and better for *everyone* takes its place. It must serve the larger tribe of humanity. This inner commitment to the larger family of man can take any form, but it must make sense to you mentally—that's the nature of an air sign. Once you commit to it, it's wholehearted commitment—that's the nature of a fixed sign.

Like Scorpio, you're stubborn and slow to change your mind, so this area is where you and your boss may run into trouble.

Using Your Strengths

As a sign ruled by Uranus, your visionary talent undoubtedly spells genius in at least one area of your life. Perhaps you're able to see through other people's masks and camouflages. Or maybe you're able to take complex abstractions and make them easy to understand. Perhaps you excel at reading patterns in nature, in people or in divination systems. Whatever your particular genius, use it!

Like your air sign sibling, Gemini, your communication skills are excellent. You can converse about a great many things and enjoy lively exchanges about ideas and concepts, ideals, politics and creativity. Scorpio will tap into these skills and will also tap into your steel-trap memory. *Hey, Aquarius, what was our target last April?* And you'll conjure up the details of the day you discussed the target, the scents in the room and who was there; and voilà, you'll have the answer.

Stand Up for What You Believe

From the choices you make as a consumer to the TV shows you watch, the movies you see, the books you read and the politicians for whom you vote, you're standing up for what you believe. You're a principled individual with a strong sense of right and wrong and a firm vision of what you want for yourself and your professional life.

It's unlikely that Scorpio will ever ask you to do something that goes against your principles, but there may be occasions when the two of you disagree on how a particular project or task should be carried out. If you feel particularly strongly that your way is the right way, be assured that Scorpio probably thinks the same thing about *his* way. And this is the place where you, as an employee, must make a decision. Is there any room for compromise?

Set Goals

In setting goals for yourself, you're able to bring greater creativity to your professional life. Yes, you may gripe and complain that you're out of new ideas, but that's just a stall for time. The truth is that once you set your sights on something, you move ahead at full steam.

Consider your goals as the overall picture and think of the time and strategy as the small picture. Start with goals you can accomplish in a day, a week or maybe as long as a month, so you can see your progress more quickly. Once you achieve these smaller goals, set larger goals for a longer time frame. In this way, you become accustomed to bringing a creative slant to your job daily.

Compatibility

Air and water signs aren't known for their compatibility. But this employee/boss relationship can be a powerful combination when you each understand the other's strengths and tap them. Here are some tips for both of you to maintain a harmonious relationship.

For Scorpio:

➤ If there's a prime directive for Aquarius, it's freedom to explore what interests him and to express his creativity in his own way. If you, as the boss, give Aquarius that freedom, you'll be ensuring that his job performance will be top-notch.

➤ In a disagreement with Aquarius, listen to his side. If you simply dismiss it with, *My way or the highway,* Aquarius may take the highway.

➤ If you feel resistance to something that Aquarius suggests, it would be to your advantage to ask where this resistance originates. Get to the root of it. Once you do that, your resistance may evaporate.

For *Aquarius:*

➢ You can be emotionally remote at times, a trait that often bewilders the people around you. It's as if you've gotten up on the wrong side of the bed and simply can't be bothered with other people. Yet, to create anything worthwhile, you must do so from a deep place. Emotions are what connect you to your muse and to your personal mythology. Strive to be more emotionally aware, Aquarius.

➢ Now read the last suggestion for Scorpio. It applies to you as well.

Keeping Scorpio Happy

Try an experiment. Ask Scorpio what makes her happiest. Then ask yourself if you can provide whatever it is.

You & Your Muse

To bring maximum creativity to your job, you'll need to summon your muse from time and time. For you, this is simple. Close your eyes and make a request. It's like what used to happen on the old TV show *I Dream of Jeannie.* The request you make is the equivalent of rubbing that magic lamp. Or, create a ritual that indicates your intent; take a walk or say a prayer. Anything that signals your intent will work. For you, creativity is also a spiritual practice.

Pisces & the Scorpio Boss

Tuned In

Your interview probably didn't last even five minutes. In you, Scorpio immediately recognized a kindred soul. He knew that the scope of your inner life was as vast as his own and that you, like him, perceived the world through the lens of your emotions and intuition. He felt that your creative talents would be a valuable asset to his company.

Water signs often have a natural affinity with each other and in an employee/boss relationship, it's a definite plus. You're able to sense what Scorpio wants or needs without any words being spoken and often sense it before Scorpio himself knows it. As a mutable water sign, you're emotionally adaptable just like your mutable cousins Gemini, Virgo and Sagittarius. You can be a chameleon and are often impossible to pigeonhole, even for someone as perceptive as Scorpio.

Using Your Strengths

Neptune, the ruler of your sign, is the astrological source of your creativity. Jupiter, which co-rules your sign, brings expansiveness to your talents. Together, these two planets enable you to create in an organic, holistic way rather than through deliberate strategies, outlines and planning. You're able to intuitively perceive the entirety of whatever you're creating and trust that it will all come out fine in the end.

Pisces, like Gemini, is a dual sign, represented by two fish swimming in opposite directions. One fish symbolizes your heart, your intuition and imagination, and the other symbolizes reason, left-brain thinking and your mind. Ideally, your creativity rises from a blend of heart and mind. Scorpio will give you plenty of freedom to do that.

Stand Up for What You Believe

Thanks to your adaptability, you're able to adjust easily to situations that are fluid and in flux. But you can sometimes be so adaptable that it's difficult for you to stand up for yourself or your beliefs. You would rather avoid conflict and be left alone. *Oops, I don't like what I see or what I have to deal with, so I'm outta here.* That's the escapist part of Neptune.

Or you vacillate, weighing one option against another. This kind of mental gymnastics goes something like this:

If I tell the truth about this, I risk getting fired.
If I remain silent, I won't be able to live with myself.
Maybe I should…
No, that won't work, either.

And round and round you go until you just can't stand it anymore and retreat into yourself.

The exception to this is when you it concerns your creativity—the process or the product. Then you'll not only stand up, you'll fight tooth and nail!

Set Goals

You generally aren't one for setting goals, at least not consciously. But when it comes to a creative approach to your job and your professional life, it's to your advantage to do so. Start with daily or weekly goals that are easily attainable. If you work as an illustrator for a magazine or book publisher, for instance, then your daily list might look something like this:

➢ Finish art for (name the project).
➢ Start art for (name it).
➢ Get approval for (name it).

Post the list in your work area. When you attain your daily goals easily, then try weekly and monthly goals. With practice, setting goals will become second nature to you.

Compatibility

Peas in a pod. Telepathic moments. Sometimes, you may even finish each other's sentences. This combination is exceptionally compatible. To maintain this harmonious relationship, here are some tips for both of you.

For Scorpio:

➤ Give Pisces his own work area where he can daydream, doodle and dive into his imagination.

➤ When you disagree on something, listen to his concerns rather than expecting him to cave just because you're the boss.

➤ Give him a flexible schedule. Is he a lark who does his best work as the sun rises? Or an owl who does his best work in the darkest part of the night? Adjust his schedule accordingly.

For Pisces:

➤ Try not to vacillate. Make a choice and follow through.

➤ When you and Scorpio disagree on something, voice your opinion. Don't just surrender to avoid conflict.

➤ Think as far outside the box as you can.

Keeping Scorpio Happy

When you're happy, you're more productive, and that makes Scorpio happy.

You & Your Muse

Your muse is the vehicle for your creativity. She comes to you in dreams, when you daydream, when you're walking, hiking or swimming. Because you live in a world of emotion and imagination, you can easily summon your muse. Maybe you only have to shut your eyes and request that she or he appear. Perhaps you have a ritual you perform that helps to summon your muse. Maybe a particular type of music or a special song is all that you need to get in touch with your muse. Whatever your method, use it frequently!

Chapter 7:

Best Buds & Colleagues

"With enough courage, you can do without a reputation."
Margaret Mitchell, November 8

Friendships are gifts that come in all shapes and sizes. Some are beautifully and carefully wrapped, others are whimsical, and some are mysterious. If you're friends with or a colleague of a Scorpio, the relationship probably isn't like others that you have.

A friend, like a colleague, is someone with whom you're equal. When sex and issues about authority and power are removed from the equation, many of the potential problems in a relationship evaporate. Regardless of whether Scorpio is male or female, the relationship possesses depth, surprises, mystery and much creative potential.

It may actually be easier for a friend or colleague to unlock the secrets to a Scorpio than it is for a partner or a spouse.

Aries & Scorpio as Friends/ Colleagues

Adventurous

Camaraderie
While it's true that we don't become friends with all our colleagues, you two may be drawn together through a love of competitive sports, a passion for a particular type of creative work or because you both prize your individual freedom. Or all of the above.

Your personality differences find a curious balance in this relationship that is lacking in other types of Aries/Scorpio affiliations. Your impatience, for instance, may prompt patient Scorpio to pick up his pace because he admires the speed at which you move and work. His patience may urge you to slow down, to mull things over a bit before you leap to a decision. This give-and-take becomes a powerful undercurrent in the relationship and you both learn from it. Scorpio learns to compromise and you learn that changing your behavior doesn't threaten who you are.

You recognize that you and Scorpio share a core trait: fearlessness.

Taboos

Most of us probably have taboos—areas of our lives we don't talk about with others, topics we avoid or traits in others that drive us crazy. Early on in this relationship, you both learned these parameters.

Aries has fewer taboos than Scorpio, but to avoid schisms in this relationship, there are a couple of areas to be avoided.

Aries Taboos That Scorpio Should Avoid

➢ Scorpio, don't question the way Aries spends money. Just because you stash away 15 percent of what you earn doesn't mean that he should, too.

➢ Don't offer your opinion on her love life. Who she dates or marries is really none of your business. Even if you dislike her partner, it's best if you keep your opinion to yourself.

➢ Don't criticize the quality of her work.

Scorpio Taboos That Aries Should Avoid

➢ Don't encroach on Scorpio's privacy. That means that if you ask him how his marriage is these days, he either won't answer or will provide a one-word response.

➢ Don't stretch the truth or lie. He'll see through it and that will be the end of the friendship.

➢ Keep your word.

➢ Think twice before you criticize something Scorpio has created. You're often blunt and impulsive when stating your opinion and that can be hurtful.

What to Expect

All of us enter into relationships with expectations of one kind or another. Some of the expectations pan out, others don't. Here are some things each of you can expect from this friendship.

From Aries

➢ Adventures. *This is my life and I'll live it the way I want.* That's the Aries battle cry. It means that no two adventures will be the same, and they'll happen on the spur of the moment. You, Scorpio, might get a call from Aries at sunrise telling you he's headed out for a five-mile bike ride and ask if you are up for it? Or he might want to know if you'd like to join him for breakfast at this great vegan restaurant he just ran across. He won't ever be offended if you say no thanks.

➢ The blunt truth. If you ask him for his opinion, he gives it. You may not always like what he says, but it will be his unvarnished truth.

➢ Fun, action, movement, restlessness and a constant drive to move forward

➢ As a colleague, you're an innovator.

From Scorpio

➢ Loyalty. Once you've earned Scorpio's trust, there is no friend more loyal.

➢ Piercing insight into who you are and what makes you tick

➢ Charisma and magnetism that attracts the attention of other people. It can be daunting to your ego, Aries, but if you value the friendship, you learn to live with it.

➢ A hard-working colleague

Taurus & Scorpio as Friends/ Colleagues

Kindred Souls

Camaraderie

With certain people you meet, something clicks immediately. You recognize a kindred spirit. That's probably how it was with you and Scorpio. It's as if this immediate camaraderie originates in some deep inner place that you both inhabit much of the time. Even though you two are considered astrological opposites, this combination works well in most relationships and usually feels comfortable if you're colleagues or friends.

Women of both signs are more inclined to talk about their feelings and personal lives. But both men and women internalize their emotions, constantly sifting through them in an attempt to understand them. However, once you and Scorpio trust each other—as colleagues or friends—the flow of communication picks up, and you begin to discover and enjoy what you have in common.

This relationship can easily evolve into a business partnership, particularly if you work in the arts or entertainment business.

Taboos

Remember the adage about still waters running deep? It fits both of you. And because you are essentially private individuals with vibrant inner lives, there are certain areas you should avoid with each other in order to keep the relationship flowing smoothly.

Taurus Taboos That Scorpio Should Avoid

➤ Scorpio, don't push Taurus for answers he isn't willing to provide. When he's ready to tell you how he feels or what he thinks about something, he'll do so.

➤ Unsolicited opinions about how he could improve his work

➤ Never take him or the friendship for granted.

➤ Avoid confrontations with him. Even though he is slow to anger, once his buttons are pushed, he blows up. It's called the bull's rush!

Scorpio Taboos That Taurus Should Avoid

➤ Don't encroach on Scorpio's privacy. You're unlikely to do this because you value your privacy as well, but be forewarned.

➤ Don't take her for granted.

➤ Don't criticize, condemn or complain, especially about the quality of her work.

What to Expect

As a pair of fixed signs, your respective expectations in this relationship are probably similar and may change and evolve over time. But here are the broad strokes on what you can expect from each other:

From Taurus

➢ Great conversations about the mysterious, the unknown, about things that go bump in the night. You, Scorpio, will delight in this part of your friendship. You're both comfortable in this terrain.

➢ Hard worker, ethical

➢ Loyalty and patience

➢ Compassion. Taurus is the person you turn to, Scorpio, when you're feeling low or encounter daunting obstacles.

➢ Pragmatism and insight into who you are

From Scorpio

➢ Loyalty and patience

➢ Hard worker, ethical

➢ A friend who listens carefully and intuitively analyzes everything you say

➢ A quest for the bottom line in whatever she tackles. In some ways, you and Scorpio are on the same page with this bottom-line stuff, Taurus. But your bottom line is how to make something useful, practical and more efficient.

Unlocking the Secret to Scorpio

Your patience and persistence are the keys to unlocking the secret to Scorpio. The friendship possesses such a strong balance that it won't take you long to fully grasp who your friend/colleague is.

Gemini & Scorpio as Friends/ Colleagues

Exciting

Camaraderie

You're fascinated by the way Scorpio probes and digs for answers and information. Scorpio is intrigued by your curiosity and by that single burning question that drives you: *why?* You're a connector and a communicator, and you collect information the way other people collect books or antiques. Scorpio may be puzzled by your diversity, your ability to talk to anyone anywhere about virtually anything. You are equally puzzled by her piercing insights into human nature.

Unless one of you has a moon or rising in the other's sun sign, this relationship may not have the profound depth of some of the other combinations. But the versatility, intellectual excitement and the exchange of ideas keep it interesting and vibrant as both friends and colleagues. Neither of you are ever quite sure what treasures the relationship might yield in a given moment, and that's no small thing.

Taboos

All of us—you, too, Gemini—have private spaces within ourselves that we don't share even with our closest friends. We have behaviors and attitudes that drive other people nuts and beliefs that may sound wacko to someone else. But the taboos we're talking about here concern who we are in relation to the other person.

Gemini Taboos That Scorpio Should Avoid

➤ Scorpio, you would be wise to never make fun of Gemini or make her the butt of a joke, particularly if you're with a group of people. That's probably at the top of her list of taboos and grounds for ending the relationship.

➤ Don't belittle her strengths—as a communicator and networker.

➤ Because her approach to life is generally more lighthearted than yours, you may sometimes think she's like a little kid whose decisions have to be scrutinized, whose math has to be checked. But be careful; few things will rile her up more quickly than this.

➤ Don't criticize her unjustly.

Scorpio Taboos That Gemini Should Avoid

Because you, Gemini, are a communicator and Scorpio is more reticent, there are certain taboos that are established early in this relationship.

➤ Talking constantly. Gemini, sometimes you talk just to fill the silence, and while Scorpio understands this, he can only take so much of it. Sometimes, he just wants to shout, *Be quiet! Let me think!*

➤ Confiding too much, too quickly, 24/7

➤ Hypocrisy

What to Expect

You're a mutable air sign and Scorpio is a fixed water sign, and one thing that means is that you won't always agree on everything. It's part of what keeps the relationship interesting and diverse. As colleagues, these disagreements help to keep ideas fresh. What else can you expect from each other in this relationship?

From Gemini

- ➢ Meeting a variety of new people. Since Gemini is a consummate networker, you'll be drawn into her circle of acquaintances and friends. An expansion of contacts is beneficial in your relationship as colleagues and keeps the friendship fresh and exciting.
- ➢ Intellectual stimulation
- ➢ Creative ideas and solutions, a must if you and Gemini are colleagues on a creative project
- ➢ A friend who listens and discusses
- ➢ Fun!
- ➢ Acceptance of who you are as both friend and colleague

From Scorpio

- ➢ In-depth knowledge about the human psyche
- ➢ Loyalty and patience
- ➢ Intuitive insight into who you are
- ➢ Great passion about whatever interests her
- ➢ Considerate friend and colleague

Unlocking the Secret to Scorpio

The best way for you to do this is by doing what you do best—communicating. Engage Scorpio in conversations about ideas, creativity, the nature of reality, the afterlife or your feelings, ideas and thoughts. Draw him out.

Cancer & Scorpio as Friends/ Colleagues

Allies

Camaraderie

BFF: that's the potential in this relationship. You and Scorpio enjoy an intuitive connection that can be downright eerie at times. If one of you is feeling down or is in trouble, the other may pick up on it. You may complete each other's sentences. Your connection can be similar to what identical twins often experience, an *inner knowing* about each other. Whether you're friends or colleagues or both, this inner knowing serves you both well.

Since you're both water signs, you experience the world through your emotions and intuition and this is true regardless of your gender. The one possible glitch in this friendship is that Scorpio's personality is so strong you may feel the need to disengage sometimes, to move off into your private space, particularly if you're roommates. You so readily feel what other people feel that your tendency to nurture and comfort may make Scorpio feel smothered. Otherwise, this combination in a friendship is nearly ideal.

Taboos

In this relationship, the taboos are probably understood without ever discussing them. But just in case you need to be reminded, here are the broad strokes for both of you.

Cancer Taboos That Scorpio Should Avoid

➤ When Cancer is in one of his moods, don't press him to explain what he feels, why he's withdrawing or what he's thinking. Most likely he just wants to be left alone.

➤ Confrontations. Cancer dislikes confrontations and will do practically anything to avoid one. If you have something to say that's confrontational, email or text him about it.

➤ Rejection. Cancer is very nurturing, and when her nurturing is rejected, she takes it personally. Find a kind way to say thanks, but no thanks.

➤ Someone trying to control her. As a colleague or friend, this shouldn't be an issue. But if it is, you're advised to find someone else to control!

➤ Dishonesty

Scorpio Taboos That Cancer Should Avoid

➤ Don't smother him! Scorpio enjoys being nurtured—who doesn't? But too much of it leaves him feeling suffocated.

➤ Dishonesty. While it's unlikely that either of you will deliberately lie, the truth is sometimes stretched so feelings aren't hurt.

➤ Not following through

➤ Clinging

What to Expect

You and Scorpio value loyalty in your friendships. But for both of you, trust must be earned. Once it is, then the friendship usually unfolds smoothly. Even in the best of friendships, though, our expectations are sometimes unrealistic, so be aware of that possibility in yourself.

From Cancer

- ➤ Nurturing
- ➤ Faith that things will work out
- ➤ Emotional highs and lows
- ➤ Cancer forgives, but he rarely forgets.
- ➤ Hard worker who follows the voice of his intuition
- ➤ Loyalty
- ➤ Intuitive insight into you and the friendship
- ➤ Life is her creative fodder.

From Scorpio

The list of what you can expect from Cancer looks almost identical to what Cancer can expect from you in this relationship.

- ➤ Scorpio forgives, but she rarely forgets.
- ➤ Creates from a need to understand himself
- ➤ Penetrating insight into you and the relationship
- ➤ Loyalty
- ➤ Blunt honesty

Unlocking the Secret to Scorpio

The best way to do this is to allow your intuition to guide you through Scorpio's layers of complexity. Be aware that she is using her intuition in figuring out who you are as well.

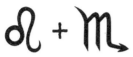

Leo & Scorpio as Friends/Colleagues

Generosity & Abundance

Camaraderie

Scorpio is enthralled with your vivaciousness, wit, generosity and creative drive. You, in turn, are intrigued by Scorpio's sheer presence, her charisma and the air of mystery around her. As a fire and water sign respectively, your approaches to life and work are vastly different, but it's this very difference that suggests the relationship won't go stale.

Your life and your relationships often involve heightened drama of some kind. It's the drama that makes you feel alive, creative and in the flow. Scorpio may not see it like that. She's really not into high drama. But as your friend, she'll listen and advise you. As a colleague, she understands that your flair for the dramatic can be integrated and channeled into the work you do together.

Taboos

Leos seem to come in two distinct varieties. One type is forthright and public about nearly everything. The other kind of Leo is more private and circumspect and generally has more areas that are off limits. Regardless of which type you are, Leos tend to take things personally. If a friend or colleague makes a remark that you perceive as critical of your creative talent or something you've produced, it may not be intended that way at all. It may just be your insecurity.

Scorpio's taboos are determined by how much she trusts you, whether the relationship is casual or close. She can take things personally, too, but her reaction is apt to be quite different from yours. No outbursts, just an abrupt withdrawal. Here are the broad strokes for both of you:

Leo Taboos That Scorpio Should Avoid
➤ Unjust criticism of his creative skills and talents
➤ *You ridiculed me!* This is a deal breaker for Leo, particularly if he's ridiculed publicly. But what friend would do that?
➤ When people don't give him their full attention, he feels anger and resentment. So be forewarned, Scorpio. Pay attention!
➤ Not being complimented, especially when it's deserved!
➤ Attempts to control him

Scorpio Taboos That Leo Should Avoid
➤ Being taken for granted
➤ Failure to recognize her contributions to a project
➤ Attempts to control her and her time
➤ Being asked repeatedly what she feels or thinks. Many times, she simply feels her way through situations and isn't able to articulate it.

What to Expect
A friendship between two fixed signs is probably easier in many respects than a marriage or partnership. Even though you're both stubborn individuals with beliefs and opinions that can be somewhat rigid, it doesn't have to be an issue in a relationship with a friend or colleague. You both work around it. So what can you and Scorpio expect in this relationship?

From Leo

- ➤ Loyalty
- ➤ Drama
- ➤ Adventure. The adventures entail the arts, theater, interior design, fashion, books and exotic ports of call.
- ➤ A love of animals
- ➤ Creativity

From Scorpio

- ➤ Loyalty
- ➤ Exploration of the unknown, the mysterious or the esoteric
- ➤ Confidentiality
- ➤ Psychological insight into who you are and what motivates you
- ➤ Unusual creative talents

Unlocking the Secret to Scorpio

Your own creativity is the key that unlocks the secret to Scorpio. When you and Scorpio are involved in a creative project together, watch how quickly that door to her inner self opens.

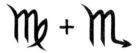

Virgo & Scorpio as Friends/Colleagues

Comfortable

Camaraderie

This relationship is as comfortable as your favorite pair of shoes. Scorpio is awed by your meticulous intellect, by the way you connect dots that he often doesn't see and by your ability to sift through information at lightning speed. You admire Scorpio's depth, intuitive insights and his ability to research and dig and probe for the answers he needs. Whatever eccentricities you both have are neatly integrated into the friendship.

The one possible rough spot in this relationship is your tendency to critique and perfect. It's one thing when it's directed at you, but Scorpio won't appreciate it when he's on the receiving end. And you may not appreciate Scorpio's analysis of your motives or his dissection of your psyche. Those things aside, this relationship is one to relish.

Taboos

Not many taboos exist in this relationship. You and Scorpio understand each other well enough to know when to back off or to move ahead, what to avoid and what is welcome or not. From an astrological perspective, it's the compatibility of earth and water that probably accounts for it. But because we all need reminders from time to time, here is the bigger picture for both of you.

Virgo Taboos That Scorpio Should Avoid
- ➤ Mean-spirited comments or sarcasm about something Virgo is doing or creating or about some facet of her personality
- ➤ Being made the butt of a joke
- ➤ Rudeness in any form
- ➤ Attempts to control her
- ➤ Lack of appreciation for her contributions as a colleague

Scorpio Taboos That Virgo Should Avoid
- ➤ Critiques about Scorpio's partner or another loved one
- ➤ Analysis of her behavior or attitude
- ➤ Obsessiveness. This one is somewhat ironic, since she can sometimes be obsessive about work, love and life itself.

What to Expect

Who can you call at four in the morning when you're in a quiet panic? Scorpio. The reverse is also true. When either of you needs a friend to unload on, you are there for each other. Compassion is intricately woven into this relationship and is the foundation for everything else that unfolds.

As a mutable sign, you're more flexible than Scorpio, and it's easier for you to adapt to a fluid situation—like a panicked call at 4:00 a.m. If you're the one who is calling Scorpio in that darkest pocket of the night, the sound of her calm voice and her reassurance that it's all going to be okay will soothe you quickly. Here are some other things you can each expect.

From Virgo
- ➤ A levelheaded approach to just about everything. In terms of the relationship as friend or colleague, Virgo can take the most abstract and esoteric topic that you talk about and make it comprehensible to others.

- ➢ Wit and humor
- ➢ Honesty and the truth as he sees it

From Scorpio
- ➢ Loyalty
- ➢ Probing questions about the nature of reality
- ➢ Intuitive knowledge and insight
- ➢ Deep reservoirs of creativity

Unlocking the Secret to Scorpio

The best way for you to do this is through your careful observation and your penchant for details. For you it's an investigation, a treasure hunt in which you connect the clues. And yes, X marks the spot!

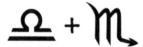

Libra & Scorpio as Friends/ Colleagues

Smooth

Camaraderie

Your life is all about relationships of one kind or another. You're here to form deep and abiding bonds that allow you to confront and deal with the dichotomies and contradictions in human nature. And in your relationship with Scorpio, there are plenty of them.

You're intrigued by Scorpio's capacity for introspection and for mining her own psyche, and you are often blown away by her intuitive perceptions. She may not always be right, but when she is, she's so on target it can be downright spooky. She, in turn, is captivated by your ability to see the many sides of any issue, situation or relationship. When she's presented with these various views it can shake her out of her singular opinions and beliefs. This relationship works on many levels.

Taboos

You and Scorpio both hunger for connections with people. *Real* connections, *deep* connections. Neither of you settle for superficiality. But your approaches to finding these deeper connections differ. Scorpio probes and digs and uses her intuition to dive deeper and deeper. You enter the flow of the friendship and allow that current to sweep you into the heart of it. Whatever taboos you both have are easily avoided.

Libra Taboos That Scorpio Should Avoid

> *I'm not a pushover!* The biggest mistake that you, Scorpio, can make in this relationship as colleague or friend is to believe that Libra will bend to your will. If you suggest heading downtown for a drink and dinner, and he dislikes the venue or the food, don't expect him to join you anyway. If you feel a project should be approached in a particular way, and he disagrees, don't get miffed.

> Unsolicited, negative comments or observations about his partner, spouse or children or his taste in music, literature or the arts

> Unsolicited opinions about his quest for balance or his approach to any creative project

Scorpio Taboos That Libra Should Avoid

> Excessive dependence on her or on the relationship

> Unsolicited observations about Scorpio's lack of trust or the defensive moat she erects around herself

What to Expect

Scorpio is always there for you, Libra. Whether it's a call in the middle or the night or a visit at dawn, Scorpio's door and heart are open to you. The reverse is also true. Libra, as a cardinal air sign, and Scorpio, a fixed water sign, possess an innate understanding of each other as friends/colleagues.

From Libra

➤ A calm presence
➤ A balanced approach
➤ An ability to feel what you feel, to slip on your shoes and walk in them
➤ Great humor that lightens the mood
➤ A loving heart

From Scorpio

➤ Insight
➤ Loyalty
➤ The bottom-line truth
➤ A sharing of resources

Unlocking the Secret to Scorpio

Engage Scorpio in your creative interests, in the music, literature and art that move you. A whole new facet of Scorpio will emerge.

Scorpio & Scorpio as Friends/Colleagues

Visceral

Camaraderie

This duo as friends or colleagues can be summed up in a single word: wow. The tremendous power in this combination may feel like destiny, like kismet, and you may even sense the past-life connections. At the very least, it's likely that you and Scorpio felt an immediate and visceral attraction and chemistry when you met. Perhaps you spent time talking about your various interests and discovered you share some of the same passions.

In a relationship between Scorpios where sex and power aren't issues, you have an opportunity for exploration that you may not have with other friends and colleagues. It might be an exploration of the nature of reality, the human psyche, the paranormal, your creative passions or the hidden side of life. The two of you might undertake a quest to some far-flung corner of the world in search of a rare manuscript or mythological creature. Your relationship might unfold like a Dan Brown novel.

One thing is certain: you won't ever be bored as friends or colleagues!

Taboos

Most of us have pet peeves of one kind or another, behaviors or attitudes that drive us bonkers, areas in our lives we don't share with just anyone. You and your Scorpio friend may have similar taboos, but they won't be identical. You're different people whose lives and personalities have been shaped and molded by your individual experiences.

In any friendship where two people share the same sun sign, it's a good idea to have your natal charts drawn up to see how you differ emotionally (the moon) and how other people perceive you (rising sign). Also, look to see in which house your respective suns fall. That's the area where you'll shine! Get your free natal chart here: http://alabe.com/freechart/.

This list of taboos for Scorpio is general. You and your Scorpio friend or colleague are probably on the same page with these pet peeves, so they won't be a problem.

Scorpio Taboos

➢ Encroachment on his privacy
➢ Pressing him for answers he isn't able or willing to give yet
➢ Anyone taking him for granted
➢ Failure to recognize his contributions on a joint project
➢ Attempts to control him
➢ Emotional manipulation
➢ Unsolicited, negative remarks or observations about his partner, spouse, children or other friends
➢ Dishonesty
➢ Hypocrisy

What to Expect

As friends and/or colleagues, like any relationship between a pair of Scorpios, emotional intensity exists. You're both passionate, independent individuals who know what you like and don't like. You may both live in an either/or world, where something is good or bad, right or wrong, positive or negative. In other words, there is no nuance, no gray area. It's part of what makes you such a formidable personality.

Given all this, what can you expect from a friendship with a fellow Scorpio?

From Scorpio
- ➢ Strong opinions and beliefs
- ➢ Loyalty once you've earned his trust
- ➢ Penetrating intuitive insights
- ➢ Honesty

Unlocking the Secret to Scorpio

Bottom line? We're all mortal. We're all going to die. Our mortality unites us at the deepest, most transformative levels, and just about everything else is a moot point. Once you understand this about yourself and your Scorpio friend, you've unlocked the secret.

Sagittarius & Scorpio as Friends/ Colleagues

Let the Good Times Roll!

Camaraderie

Of all the possible types of relationships, that of colleagues and/or friends is the easiest for this combination. There aren't any complications with sex, power or the kinds of obligations that exist in a marriage, partnership or a parent/child relationship. It's as if this relationship allows you and Scorpio to enjoy the best in each other.

You're fascinated by Scorpio's perceptions, his uncanny ability to see details that you miss, to penetrate to the heart of a situation and to interpret metaphor and symbols. He admires your unquenchable thirst for *experience,* the largesse of your personality and your ability to get up and go at a moment's notice. And you have a mutual admiration for each other's creativity.

Even if you start out as friends, the relationship could easily morph into a partnership where you join forces to write a book or a screenplay or to spearhead some sort of grassroots project about which you're both passionate. You can see the big picture of this project, Sadge, and Scorpio sees the bottom line. Now: how are you two going to get from A to Z?

Taboos

Most of us have private spaces we don't readily share with others, pet peeves and behaviors that irritate us. Scorpio probably has more private spaces than you do, Sadge, but you may outdo her in the pet peeves/irritating behaviors department. Not everything on the bulleted list will apply to you or Scorpio. It depends on whether you are friends or colleagues.

Sagittarius Taboos That Scorpio Should Avoid

> *I am who I am!* If each of us has a battle cry, then this is Sadge's. It makes him nuts when people try to psychoanalyze him, particularly in a negative way. Scorpio, you may do this more than other signs and would be wise to back off doing it with him.

> When someone tries to stifle his personal freedom, it's grounds for ending the relationship.

Scorpio Taboos That Sagittarius Should Avoid

Sadge, it's unlikely that you will ask Scorpio repeatedly what she feels and why, or that you'll question her loyalty as a friend. You aren't likely to violate her privacy, either. So what are the taboos in this friendship?

- She can't abide being told that her truth is false. She may be guilty of this as well with you, but you'll let it roll away. She won't.
- Unsolicited opinions about something she has created or about her partner, spouse or children.

What to Expect

As a nomadic, freedom-loving Sadge, you have a large network of acquaintances, friends and colleagues that probably reaches around the planet. You're always enthusiastic about adding to that network. Scorpio, of course, has her own network. Wouldn't it be interesting to find out what happens when these two vastly different networks combine forces?

Here's what each of you can expect from the other in this friendship:

From Sagittarius

- A worldview that is dramatically different from yours. Thanks to the expansiveness of Jupiter, which rules Sagittarius, Sadge's approach to life and living is externally broader than yours.
- Optimism, an upbeat attitude
- A unique approach to creativity
- Fun and adventure. Like her fire sign cousin, Aries, she's all about movement, action and experience.
- Creative solutions

From Scorpio

- Honesty
- Loyalty
- A broad inner perspective
- Intuitive astuteness

Capricorn & Scorpio as Friends/ Colleagues

Focus

Camaraderie

In some ways, you're as serious-minded as Scorpio and just as private, although for different reasons. With Scorpio, privacy may be a defense mechanism; for you, it's simply what you prefer. The better you and Scorpio get to know each other, whether as friends or colleagues, the greater the trust that grows between you and the deeper you'll penetrate into each other's privacy.

Scorpio admires your steady, tenacious, dependable nature, your discipline and your ability to set goals and achieve them. You recognize that Scorpio possesses these same traits, but the two of you may be motivated for different reasons. You aspire to create or be involved in something that makes a difference in the world; Scorpio aspires to find that bottom line, to understand what makes everything tick.

A powerhouse of energy, focus, determination and ambition marks this relationship. When the two of you combine forces on any kind of creative project, there's no telling where it might lead or what it might produce.

Taboos

The privacy issue isn't likely to be an issue in this friendship because you're both on the same page in this regard. The only taboos you may encounter have to do with the darker facets of your respective signs.

The shadow side of your sign, Capricorn, is that the ends justify the means. It's naked ambition, that all encompassing drive that urges you forward toward some pinnacle of achievement, and it doesn't matter who you trample to get there. The shadow side for Scorpio is about obsessive control of her environment and everything in it. Here are some minor taboos/pet peeves you may want to keep in mind.

Capricorn Taboos That Scorpio Should Avoid
- ➤ Not receiving the recognition she feels she deserves
- ➤ When someone else takes credit for work she's done
- ➤ Questioning her integrity

Scorpio Taboos That Capricorn Should Avoid
- ➤ Being expected to do something he really doesn't want to do
- ➤ Adhering to rules that aren't his rules and that he believes don't serve a purpose
- ➤ Interruptions when he's deeply focused

What to Expect

Since you two are similar in the ways that count in a friendship, you can depend on each other to do what you say you'll do. That's a big deal for both of you. What else can you expect from each other?

From Scorpio

- ➤ Loyalty
- ➤ Honesty
- ➤ Emotional support
- ➤ Creative suggestions/solutions
- ➤ Profound discussions about the esoteric, the mysterious and the unknown and about the nature of life—and of death

From Capricorn

- ➤ Pragmatism and efficiency
- ➤ Loyalty
- ➤ Emotional support
- ➤ Goal orientation

Unlocking the Secret to Scorpio

Observation, analysis and allowing yourself to connect on an intuitive level with Scorpio. It sounds simpler than it actually is, though, and will require patience. But you generally have an abundance of patience!

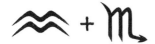

Aquarius & Scorpio as Friends/Colleagues

Visionary

Camaraderie

As friends or colleagues, this relationship has several outstanding strengths. You're the visionary of the zodiac, Aquarius, the one who spots cutting edge trends before anyone else. Scorpio appreciates just how valuable this ability is in the work you two do. He takes this visionary information and tests it against his intuitive barometer. If it feels right, he runs with it. This process is essential to a team working toward the same goal—a product or service that will compete in the market.

In a friendship, this combination also works well. You're a paradigm buster, Aquarius, who seeks your own truth. In that search, you come up against the status quo and find it lacking in some way, so you break through it to something that serves the larger world in a more just way. Scorpio is a transformer who works from the inside out to bring about change in his personal world and in the larger world. You're both after the same end result; you simply have different ways of getting there. You each bring a unique slant to the friendship.

Taboos

As a pair of fixed signs, you and Scorpio are notoriously slow for changing your opinions and beliefs, and neither of you is proficient at compromise. Since you probably already understand this about each other, you avoid areas that might trigger a potential conflict—like politics and religion. But what about other pet peeves?

Aquarius Taboos That Scorpio Should Avoid

➢ *Don't tell me I'm wrong.* Aquarius knows she's not always right, but she can't abide being told so by anyone. She prefers to discover this on her own, in her own way and in her own time.

➢ She dislikes being told she can't do something or that she has to do it in a particular way, at a particular time. The freedom to call her own shots is of paramount importance to her.

➢ Questioning her loyalty to a person, relationship or cause.

Scorpio Taboos That Aquarius Should Avoid

➢ Restricted freedom. This pet peeve of Scorpio's is less likely to happen with you as a friend or colleague, but bears mentioning just in case you sometimes get careless.

➢ Unsolicited, negative remarks about anyone or anything Scorpio holds near and dear.

➢ Being rushed.

What to Expect

This section is less about expectations than it is about what you can count on with Scorpio and vice versa. Yes, air and water signs see themselves and the world through a different lens—intellect and emotion—but that shouldn't be a problem. You bring diverse strengths to the relationship.

From Aquarius

➢ An endless fount of ideas, possibilities and *what-if* scenarios

➢ Someone who usually completes what he starts. No one can ever accuse him of being a quitter!

➢ Loyalty and vision

➢ Curiosity

➢ Precision

From Scorpio

- ➢ Persistence
- ➢ Loyalty
- ➢ Honesty
- ➢ Creativity
- ➢ Hard worker

Unlocking the Secret to Scorpio

Regardless of whether you and Scorpio are friends or colleagues or both, you're able to unlock the secret to Scorpio through your intellect and visionary talent. When you engage Scorpio in your various passions, she quickly discovers that, hey, those passions speak to her! Or you teach her how to read divination systems—the tarot, the I Ching or the language of symbols.

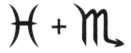

Pisces & Scorpio as Friends/ Colleagues

Imagine

Camaraderie

This relationship is like coming home. You feel relieved, secure, appreciated and at peace—well, most of the time!

As friends or colleagues or both, you and Scorpio view your experiences and yourselves through the lens of your emotions and intuition. Scorpio is usually more intense than you, and you are probably more indecisive. But these traits and behaviors are easier to work around in this relationship than in a marriage or partnership.

As colleagues, you bring your considerable imagination and intuition to anything you do, and Scorpio brings persistence and a fierce determination. When you join forces, the ideas, solutions and products you create surprise even you! As friends, you are supportive of each other and share deep bonds that are beneficial to both of you. The one possible rough spot in this relationship is Scorpio getting bossy and you capitulating to whatever he wants because it's easier than arguing about it.

Taboos

You're so sensitive to other people's moods that your pet peeves generally revolve around your emotions. You can't tolerate being around negative, morose people whose entire lives seemed to be mired in *oh woe is me.* You feel compassion for these individuals, but have learned—or will learn!—to detach yourself emotionally from them. What other taboos do you have?

Pisces Taboos That Scorpio Should Avoid
- Not being appreciated
- Unjust criticism of a creative project
- Being made fun of when she's indecisive

Scorpio Taboos That Pisces Should Avoid
- Unsolicited critique of her family, partner or kids or of something she's produced
- Constant analysis of emotions
- Endless chatter

What to Expect

In any relationship, it's important to know what you can count on with the other person. Is your Scorpio friend/colleague dependable? Loyal? Trustworthy? Responsible? Does Scorpio look for creative solutions? Is he or she a complainer? A whiner? Scorpio is also asking the same questions about you.

From Pisces

➢ Compassion
➢ Loyalty
➢ Terrific imagination and creativity
➢ Finely honed intuition
➢ Humor
➢ Gentleness
➢ Relentless work ethic when a deadline looms

From Scorpio

➢ Intuitive insight into what makes you tick
➢ Hard worker
➢ Loyalty
➢ Decisiveness
➢ Deep founts of creativity

Unlocking the Secret to Scorpio

Your intuition, which in some Pisces is outright psychic ability, is the best way to unlock the secret to Scorpio. By delving into Scorpio's personality and psyche intuitively, you discover elements that your reasoning mind missed.

Chapter 8:

Scorpio's Boundless Creativity

"Patience, persistence and perspiration make an unbeatable combination for success."
Napoleon Hill, October 26

When you hear the word *creative*, who or what comes to mind? Do you immediately think of Da Vinci? Frida Kahlo? Beethoven? Steve Jobs? Paul McCartney? Mikhail Baryshnikov? Marie Curie? Meryl Streep? Robert De Niro? Nikola Tesla? Philip K. Dick? Edith Wharton? In Western culture, we tend to think of creative people as artists, musicians, writers, actors, scientists and celebrities who have the money, time and resources to be, well, *creative.*

But creativity isn't the exclusive domain of any profession or type of individual, and it doesn't require a particular level of income. It cuts across boundaries of gender, race, religion, culture and creeds. It's about finding what you love and committing to it. It's about becoming who you are so you can realize your potential. To a great degree, your potential is described by your sun sign, that archetypal bundle of talents, traits and passions that characterize you as surely as your DNA.

One misconception about creativity is that you have to produce something *extraordinary*—a song or book, a painting, a sculpture, an invention—that will change or beautify the world and immortalize you. Yet, creativity is also about how we live from month to month, day to day, hour to hour and moment to moment. It's about creating the life we want from the inside out, through our emotions, intentions and core beliefs. "Creativity, like breathing," wrote Julia Cameron in *Vein of Gold*, "always comes down to the question, 'Are you doing it now?'"

Scorpios are beautifully equipped to create the lives they desire.

Look Around

If you want to know how you're doing in the creativity/manifestation department, take a look around. What do you see in your life? Are you happy? Miserable? Or somewhere in between? Are your relationships stable? Fulfilling? Do you like where you live? What about your job/career? Are you satisfied with where you are in your life right now? Your world isn't just a reflection of your emotions, intentions and core beliefs; it's what you *created*.

Let's say that you would like to make more money. A lot more money. How would you go about this? The first step is to pay attention to how you think and talk about money, which often reveals your core beliefs. Here are some of the most typical negative beliefs people have about money:

> ➤ I'll never make enough money.
> ➤ Money is the root of all evil.
> ➤ Rich people aren't very nice.
> ➤ Other people have all the luck with money.
> ➤ I'm not deserving.
> ➤ I'm not smart enough to make a lot of money.
> ➤ Money doesn't grow on trees.

Once you identify the core beliefs that may be holding you back, start practicing visualization and affirmations. Back both with strong emotion. This process could entail creating an affirmation that you say a hundred times a day—I am rich, I am deserving—and seeing yourself as a person who is rich. Imagine what it would feel like, what you would do, how it would improve your life and the lives of the people around you. Make these visualizations so vivid that it's as if you are already wealthy. Each day, do something that signals the universe you're ready to be wealthy. This could be something as simple as leaving a large tip at a restaurant or buying yourself an item that is more expensive than what you usually purchase.

This process, this technique, can work with anything: finding your soul mate, a career and job you love, healing yourself, making great friends, getting your novel or book published, winning an award or getting pregnant. There are a number of excellent books on how to do this. Louise Hay's classic, *You Can Heal Your Life,* is one of the best. Joe Dispenza's *You Are the Placebo* explains the science behind these techniques. Lynn Grabhorn's *Excuse Me, Your Life Is Waiting* focuses on the power of our emotions. In the book *Think and Grow Rich,* Scorpio Napoleon Hill explores the power of thought and belief in creating anything, not just wealth.

As a parent, boss, employee, friend or colleague, lover or partner, how can Scorpios tap into the creativity of the people around them? And how can others tap into Scorpio's creative energy?

Aries, the Trailblazer

You're a trailblazer, an explorer, part of a fearless group that discovers new worlds, new ways of doing things, new approaches and new ideas. Your burning desire to know what lies beyond your neighborhood, town, state and country propels you ever forward. It's a need so deep you can't ignore it, and pity the soul who attempts to hold you back.

Imagine the Orion spacecraft in late 2014 as it blasted off for its first journey into space, 3,600 miles above earth. It was propelled upward with bone-shattering force and blazed a trail into the blackness of space. Its three booster cores were 134 feet long, 17 feet wide. Each had an RS-68 engine that used liquid hydrogen and liquid oxygen propellant that produced 656,000 pounds of thrust. The Delta IV boosters collectively generated 1.96 million pounds of thrust. This is you when you're in high creative gear, filled with the most volatile energy imaginable, fire, and you mow down whatever is in your path.

Due to the innate restlessness and versatility of your sign, many of you tackle more than one area of creativity. In 1980, Aries Marilyn Ferguson published *The Aquarian Conspiracy*, which helped launch the New Age and became a best seller. Then she established the *Brain/Mind Bulletin*, a newsletter that explored the nature of consciousness. Vincent van Gogh produced some of his best work in spurts of feverish frenzies. During the two years he lived in Paris with his brother, Theo, he produced 200 paintings and sketches. In less than fifteen months, when van Gogh lived in Arles, he produced another 200 paintings.

How can Scorpio tap into such creative power? And how can you tap into Scorpio's creative energy so that you don't burn out so quickly?

Tapping In

The nature of your relationship with Scorpio will determine, to a large extent, how this creative exchange might work. The approach of a Scorpio boss, for instance, would differ from that of a parent, lover, friend or colleague.

Aries and Scorpio Tapping into Each Other's Creativity

You're a self-starter, an entrepreneur, Aries. You're terrific at generating ideas and have the enthusiasm and excitement for launching them and getting things off the ground. But Scorpio has patience that you lack; so let him finish what you start. This tenet is true across the board, regardless of your relationship with Scorpio.

For a Scorpio parent, this could mean, for example, that your Aries kid, little entrepreneur that she is, has this fantastic idea for setting up a neighborhood lemonade stand. Freshly squeezed lemons, too. She has even made signs that she posts around the neighborhood. The first week is an outstanding success. Your little Aries rakes in more than she is paid for her weekly allowance. But then she's on to the next idea, the next adventure, and the Scorpio parent has to clean up after her and figure out what to do with all the unused lemons!

If you and Scorpio are lovers or married, the scenario might go something like this. Aries, the husband, really wants to visit Greece. It's been on his bucket list for years. He knows every town, village and ruin that he absolutely must see. The trip, the way he sees it, will last two weeks. Yes, yes, the two of you are going to do this!

His excitement is infectious—until the Scorpio wife looks at the itinerary and nearly falls off her chair. The Aries itinerary calls for visiting a new place about every twelve hours. He has supersized everything. So Scorpio, of course, starts researching, digging for more information, looking for that bottom line. She pares down the itinerary by finding several central locations from which they can visit all the major cities and ruins that her supersizing Aries husband wants to see. And actually, she's thrilled by the prospect of visiting Greece, not a place that had been on her radar until now.

Perhaps Aries and Scorpio are friends, and Scorpio has an idea for a self-help book. His schedule is tight right now, though, so Aries, who loves the idea, runs with it. He churns the book out in a few months of feverish work and turns it over to Scorpio, who goes to work on it. Before Scorpio is finished going through the first draft, Aries is on to something else.

This exchange, where each person capitalizes on the other's strengths, is when the flow of creativity is at its best.

Taurus, the Practical Mystic

It sounds like something of an oxymoron. But there's no other term for a pragmatic earth sign with the soul of a poet. You hear music in your blood, feel color in your bones and see language as a flowing tide. You're a mystic in disguise who takes the abstract and the etheric and cultivates it, works with it until you bring shape and form to it and, ultimately, make it practical.

Thanks to Venus, your ruler, your aesthetic sense is finely honed, and wherever you live and work is probably a reflection of that. Because nature and its beauty are important to you, it's likely that you have created a little Walden in your personal environment, a place in the midst of urban life where you can walk, meditate and let your muse run free. Taurus George Lucas not only created beloved characters like Indiana Jones but several of the most successful movie franchises ever. He also created his private paradise at Skywalker Ranch, which sits on 2,000 acres in northern California, surrounded by redwood forests and rolling hills.

How can Scorpio tap into this sort of creative power? And how can you tap into Scorpio's creativity?

Tapping In

The nature of your relationship with Scorpio will determine, to a large extent, how this creative exchange might work. The approach of a Scorpio boss, for example, would differ from that of a parent, lover, friend or colleague.

Taurus and Scorpio Tapping into Each Other's Creativity

You and Scorpio are both stubborn individuals, and that stubbornness is intrinsic to your creativity. It's the platform from which you create. You see how something might be and then slowly and meticulously transform it into a thing of beauty that is also practical.

Let's say that as a Scorpio parent, you're a bit mystified by your Taurus son's insistence on planting a garden. But because he's so stubborn about wanting to do this, you indulge him. Seeds, soil, shovel and the proper spot with enough sunlight. And then he goes to work, step by step. By the end of the summer, his garden has produced fresh fruits and veggies for the family dinner table and that corner of the yard has been transformed into a lush beauty that probably includes a winding path and even spots where you can sit and enjoy nature. It's attracted birds and butterflies and perhaps even sprites and magical fairies!

Perhaps you and Scorpio are married and are searching for a home to buy. You have a certain amount of money to put toward the down payment. You really want a place with some land, but Scorpio would like to be on the water—a lake, a river or the ocean. You can't afford a place with both land *and* water. Since neither of you has mastered the art of compromise, your search seems to have reached a dead end.

But then Scorpio follows a creative nudge on her way home from work and finds herself in a neighborhood where she has never been. She spots a place in foreclosure, the yard overgrown with weeds, the front door hanging by a single hinge and the fence collapsing. But the place sits on an acre of land that backs up to a small lake. Scorpio knows the house needs a ton of work, but feels that you need to see it.

And you, Taurus, immediately see the place as it *might be*—a yard filled with trees and flowerbeds, a small pier that could jut out into the lake. As you're visualizing all this, Scorpio is inspecting everything that has to be fixed or replaced, what she knows she can do and what she'll have to hire someone else to do. The calculator in her brain is adding it all up. She suddenly announces, "We can afford it!"

This kind of creative exchange is the way we improve the quality of our lives, expand our intuitive capacity and find practical solutions that also seem to be endowed with a touch of mystery and magic.

♊ Gemini, the Communicator/ Networker

Since you and Pisces are the only two signs symbolized by two of something—in your case, the twins—you have two creative themes. As a communicator you're all over the place—writing, speaking and social media. Your curiosity is legendary and leads you into some strange and mysterious places. You're here to sample a banquet of experiences and then to communicate what you discover. You're always eager to share what you know and to hear what other people know. You don't even care if the stories, information and answers make sense or fit into any kind of linear timeline. When you need to, you'll make sense of it all by finding the common thread.

Gemini Whitley Strieber started out as a novelist. His vampire novel, *The Hunger,* became a film in which Susan Sarandon played one of her first roles and is now considered something of an underground classic. In the 1980s, with five novels published, Strieber turned to nonfiction. *Communion* is a personal story about his alleged abduction by non-human entities. The book was rejected by twelve publishers, and he was advised to publish the book as fiction. Eventually, it was bought for an advance of $1 million, became a best seller and was followed by several other non-fiction works.

In his dual career as non-fiction writer and novelist, the common thread throughout is typical for a Gemini: *Why? What are these entities? Why is this happening to me? Communion* launched a movement to investigate the UFO and abduction phenomena, and suddenly, UFO books had their own spots in bookstores. In a sense, Strieber's questions about UFOs and abductions, possible government knowledge and cover-ups and access to information in a free society address much larger questions about the nature of reality.

When the Internet took off, Strieber reacted in true Gemini fashion. His website, Unknown Country, is one of the best of its kind and continues the explorations begun in his books. His weekly podcast, Dreamland, features researchers and authors who explore anomalous phenomena.

How can Scorpio tap into this energetic creative flow? And how can you tap into Scorpio's creativity?

Tapping In

The nature of your relationship with Scorpio will determine how this creative exchange might work. The approach of a Scorpio parent would differ from that of a friend, lover or boss.

Gemini and Scorpio Tapping into Each Other's Creativity

Let's take a *what-if* scenario here and see how it might play out to maximize your respective creative skills.

You and Scorpio are colleagues who work in the health care industry. Scorpio learns something disturbing about one of the products that the company carries. He goes to his boss, who insists there's nothing to worry about. The company knows what they're doing, the boss says. The products go through years of testing, and everything has the bureaucratic stamp of approval.

But because Scorpio's psychic antenna continues to twitch, he digs deeper; he *knows* something is seriously wrong. He confides in you, his Gemini colleague. It turns out that you've heard some rumors to this effect, a piece of information you filed away in that steel-trap mind of yours. Now, suddenly, you understand the connection. You and Scorpio join forces and find tangible evidence that backs up his intuitive certainty.

Now what? If you become whistleblowers, you'll lose your jobs or go to jail. Or both. You, Gemini, tap into your network and are led to an investigative journalist. You and Scorpio agree to send your evidence to him. And when the case blows wide open, heads roll.

In this *what-if* scenario, you and Scorpio drew on your respective creative talents, followed your moral compasses and maybe even learned what it was like to live like spies!

Cancer, the Empath

The dictionary defines empathy as the ability to feel what others feel. Few signs do this as well as you do, Cancer. Part of it is that you are so attuned to emotions—your own and those of other people—that you're able to feel what they feel. When they hurt, you hurt. When they feel joyful, so do you. It's this ability, this innate talent, that serves as the platform for your creativity.

The ruler of your sign, the moon, governs our emotions, our inner lives and our capacity to nurture and be nurtured. So you came into this life finely attuned to the flowing river of emotions that runs through all of us. You can easily step into this current, zip yourself up inside someone else's skin and understand their world and their perceptions through what they feel. You intuit who and what they are.

Cancer Tom Hanks is one of the best examples of how individuals of this sign can funnel their emotional sensitivity into a creative endeavor. He doesn't just act; he becomes the character he portrays. In *Philadelphia,* Hanks played Andrew Beckett, a gay attorney fired from his law firm when he's diagnosed with AIDS. Hanks the man vanishes inside the skin of the character he portrays. Not surprisingly, he won an Oscar for this film.

In the 1994 film *Forrest Gump* Hanks plays a man of minimal intelligence who is present at many pivotal moments in history. He plays this character with such authenticity that, once again, Hanks the man vanishes. He won an Oscar for this role, too.

So how can Scorpio tap into your powerful creativity and vice versa?

Tapping In

The nature of your relationship with Scorpio will determine how this creative exchange might work. The approach of a Scorpio parent would differ from that of a friend, lover, boss or colleague.

Cancer and Scorpio Tapping into Each Other's Creativity

Tapping into each other's creativity should actually be easy for a pair of water signs. When you two are really attuned to each other, you probably don't even have to talk out loud. A look or a gesture is all that's needed to establish that telepathic connection.

Let's say that you and Scorpio are friends who have a terrific idea for a novel. Where to start? Do you need an outline? What kind of novel is it? Who should write what? You already have some ideas about the characters and write up bios on all of them. Scorpio has some ideas about the plot, the intrigue and the suspense and outlines the various plot points. You email back and forth. Since you're both voracious readers, you have a good sense for pacing, plot twists and surprises.

Once you've got your characters and the plot fleshed out, you realize it's time to start writing. You and Scorpio decide that you should take the first stab at the preliminary chapters and then email the material to Scorpio. So one evening you sit down on your back porch with your laptop, the bios and the outline, and stare at the blank screen. *What's my first line?* You don't know. The cursor on the blank screen blinks and blinks. The screen goes dark, and hours pass, but you still haven't found your first line. A quiet panic grips you. You call Scorpio.

"Oh my God, I don't know what the first line is."

Scorpio hears the panic in your voice. He says, "You're in a bookstore. You pick up a novel with a compelling cover, read the back copy and decide the book sounds interesting. You open it and read the first paragraph. If that paragraph grabs you, you buy the book."

Cancer quotes part of the opening paragraph of *A Tale of Two Cities*: "'It was the best of times, it was the worst of times, it was the age of wisdom, it was the age of foolishness, it was the epoch of belief, it was the epoch of incredulity...' Seriously, if I didn't know anything about the book and read that opening paragraph, I'd return it to the shelf."

And suddenly, you and Scorpio explode with laughter. "Exactly," Scorpio says. "We can do better than that."

Better than Dickens? But you're calmer now and after you hang up, you conjure the face of your protagonist—the slant of her cheekbones, the color of her eyes and the shape of her mouth. Then you step into her skin, into that current of her emotions, and suddenly, your fingers are speeding across the keyboard. You're feeling what she feels; you're channeling her. The first chapter pours out of you.

Ideally, this is how the creative exchange between you and Scorpio works. Scorpio knew exactly what to say to calm you down. Laughter broke up your panic, and you were then able to move forward. Once Scorpio had the first chapter, she increased the emotional tension and the suspense. She dove deeper into the character and carried that intensity into chapter two.

Oh, and a year later, the novel sold for six figures!

Leo, the Performer

All of us have two faces—the face that stares back at us in the mirror and the persona we present to the world. But for you, Leo, the border between the two is porous and fluid because your creative platform is performance. When you're *on,* when you're in that creative flow, only the persona exists, the archetype of the performer. This doesn't necessarily mean that your *life* is public, an open book for any stranger to page through. After all, even when you're *on,* you retain a clear sense of who you are.

As a fixed fire sign ruled by the sun, you're endowed with a natural optimism and buoyant disposition that creates a magnetism and charisma that others find irresistible. It's this optimism and trust in the process of life that allows your creative thrust to move through you like a force of nature. One way or another, it needs an outlet, and sometimes that outlet lies in the mini-dramas you create. But even mini-dramas can be useful fodder.

Leo Carl Jung wasn't just a psychologist and therapist you consulted when your life was in disarray. He mined his patients' dreams and experiences for the symbols common to all people and allowed his natural ability to lead him into a lifelong study of symbolism in mythology, folklore, primitive cultures and paranormal phenomena. As a result, he developed his theories of synchronicity, archetypes and the collective unconscious.

How can you and Scorpio tap into each other's creative talents and skills?

Tapping In

The nature of your relationship with Scorpio will determine how this creative exchange might work. The approach of a Scorpio boss would differ from that of a friend, lover, parent or colleague.

Leo and Scorpio Tapping into Each Other's Creativity

For a fire and water sign, this creative exchange can be challenging. But once you learn the ropes, the process unfolds with greater ease, and the end result will probably surprise both of you.

Let's say you're a Scorpio mother with a Leo daughter in her early teens, a time that is typically challenging for parents. Her social calendar is jammed; she has more friends than you've made in your entire life, and every day there's a new mini-drama of some kind.

Leo daughter: *My boyfriend flirted with that new girl in my math class. Then he denied doing it even though I was sitting right there and saw the whole thing. How could he do such a thing? Doesn't he like me anymore?*

Scorpio mom: *The problem is that you're both fourteen. Just don't go out with him anymore.*

Leo daughter (aghast): *What? Don't go out with him? That's nuts! He's the most popular guy in school, he says he loves me, he says…*

Mom knows this mini-drama will end with her daughter sobbing in her bedroom or inviting all her female friends to the house so they can discuss the boyfriend and gossip about the new girl. She also understands her daughter has tremendous talent that needs to find expression. She quickly changes the subject and asks if she would like to take acting lessons or learn to play the guitar or if she would like to enter that horse-jumping competition in town. The lure of *performing* serves as the necessary distraction to halt the mini-drama in its tracks. The daughter is so excited about the prospect that her optimism and buoyancy kick in again.

Perhaps the Leo daughter chooses acting lessons and ends up auditioning for admission to a theater arts school for the following school year. She gets in, and suddenly, her life has found its creative groove. For the

Scorpio mom, this game changer has impacted her life, too. She becomes involved in the theater arts program and perhaps ends up managing her daughter's acting career.

Regardless of your relationship with Scorpio, the creative exchange is triggered by your need to perform, and Scorpio's need to find that good ol' bottom line.

Virgo, the Perfectionist

As the absolute master of details, your creative theme could also be Pattern Master or Analyst. Your need for perfection really is what drives you from the inside out. It's your creative platform, your launch pad, and regardless of what you create, the end result must serve some larger, practical purpose.

If you're a writer, for instance, then the end result must first and foremost satisfy you at every level of your being. It must also entertain and inform your readers and help you to earn your living. If you're a gourmet cook, then the act of creating delectable meals must be joyful for you and enjoyed by the people who consume the food. In this sense, your focus on practicality differs from that of your earth sign brother, Taurus, for whom pragmatism is about making the abstract comprehensible.

Because your inner critic is such a busy bee, your beliefs about your creative potential are vital to your success in being innovative in every area of your life.

"What we think about ourselves and about life becomes true for us," wrote Louise Hay, author, intuitive and founder of Hay House publishing company. "I believe that everyone … is responsible for everything in our lives, the best and the worst. Every thought we think is creating our future … The thoughts we think and the words we speak create our experiences."

The significance of this statement is astonishing and probably resonates for you, Virgo, precisely because you are so deeply aware of your conscious mind.

Virgo Max Perkins has been called the greatest editor of the twentieth century. He seemed to be able to see a finished work in a way that his writers could not. With his gift for details and perfection, he helped to shape the talents and novels of some of the most famous writers—Hemingway, Fitzgerald, Marjorie Kinnan Rawlings, Taylor Caldwell and Tom Wolfe.

So how can you and Scorpio tap into each other's creativity?

Tapping In

The nature of your relationship with Scorpio will determine how this creative exchange might work. The approach of a Scorpio colleague would differ from that of a friend, lover, spouse or parent.

Virgo and Scorpio Tapping into Each Other's Creativity

As an earth and water sign, the creative exchange between the two of you should be effortless. Scorpio intuits the larger picture, and you connect the dots.

Let's say you're the father of a Scorpio child in fifth grade. Your little Scorpio absolutely loves science, especially biology, but is bored silly in every other class. As a result of his boredom, he's disruptive in the other classes. His grades are falling, and you're called in for a conference with several of his teachers. You listen quietly to the teachers' complaints, absorbing all the information, sifting through it and connecting dots.

That evening, when you and your son walk the dog around the neighborhood, you discuss the conference you had with his teachers. Instead of threatening to take away something he enjoys until his grades improve, instead of getting angry, you ask him what he would like to do about the situation. He looks at you as though he suspects it might be a trick question, but when he realizes your question is sincere, he's blunt. "I want to be a biologist. Everything else bores me."

"But everything else is a component of being a biologist," you explain. "You need to be able to read and understand what you read. You'll have to write up reports for scientific journals. You'll need math to figure out the sizes of animal habitats and how far they travel in a day."

As you connect the dots for him, a light goes off in his eyes. "I'd like to go to a school where biology is the main thing and the rest of that stuff is taught like you just explained it."

He's your diamond in the rough, right? You decide to have him tested. It turns out that his IQ falls in the superior range, and his math and science skills are practically off the charts. He's qualified for a gifted program in science, and even though it entails a commute, you enroll him. He flourishes.

And hey, who knows? He may grow up to become the next Steve Irwin!

Libra, the Peace Maker

There are several other words that would fit your creative platform—Harmonizer, Mediator—but Peace Maker really fits the ticket. Because you're able to see the many sides of a given issue, you're able to find the common ground that could even unite a room filled with warring politicians!

Part of this gift stems from your own struggle to achieve peace, harmony and balance in your life without compromising who you are or what you desire. As a cardinal air sign, you're capable of tremendous focus and the singular pursuit of a creative passion. But to do that, you sometimes just have to get out of your own mind and let the universe do its things, Libra. This requires certain vigilance about the thoughts you think and the words you utter because both thoughts and words are indicators of your core beliefs.

It took Libra Frank Herbert six years to research and write *Dune*, a perfect example of Libra's ability to stay focused on a singular path. The world Herbert created had its own unique mythology, language, rituals and customs that were written about in such beautiful and exquisite detail that when you read *Dune,* you are *there.* The book was rejected twenty-three times, finally sold for $7,500 and went on to sell nearly 30 million copies worldwide. It also became a successful movie franchise.

How can you and Scorpio tap into each other's creative energy?

Tapping In

The nature of your relationship with Scorpio will determine how this creative exchange might work. The approach of a Scorpio parent would differ from that of a friend, lover, spouse or boss.

Libra and Scorpio Tapping into Each Other's Creativity

One of the best examples of this creative exchange is the story included in Chapter 5 on Scorpio kids with Libra mom Carol Bowman and her Scorpio son Chase. Re-read that story.

It illustrates how a Libra mother who desperately needed to resolve the terrifying aversion her son had developed to fireworks took a totally unconventional approach to find answers. Even though Chase was barely five years old, he seemed to grasp the profound significance of what was happening to him. So when the hypnotist asked Chase to sit in his mother's lap, shut his eyes and talk about what he was seeing, he instinctively knew what to do. And suddenly, he was *there*, on a Civil War battlefield, describing what he saw and felt and heard.

Their creative exchange and everything that followed was so profound that it changed the course of Carol's life and freed Chase from what might have become a crippling fear that he could have carried into adulthood. This kind of Libra/Scorpio dynamic is what creativity is really about. We dive head first into the primordial soup of signs and symbols and not only alter the course of our own lives, but help to usher in a new paradigm, a new way of thinking about and perceiving the nature of reality.

♏

Scorpio, the Transformer

When you Google "The Transformers," you receive numerous links to a franchise that apparently began with a 1986 movie that was based on an animated TV series of the same name. Or you get a link to the movie, *Transformers*, released in 2007. According to IMDB, this movie was about "an ancient struggle between two Cybertronian races, the heroic Autobots and the evil Decepticons, comes to Earth, with a clue to the ultimate power held by a teenager."

Huh?

Or you find a link about how in 2014, *Transformers: Age of Extinction* made more than a billion bucks worldwide at the box office but had seven nominations in that year's Razzie nominations, which included worst picture and screenplay. Rather humbling, to say the least.

All of this actually underscores the problem with the word *transformer*. If you look it up in the dictionary, the literal meaning is straightforward: an apparatus for reducing or increasing the voltage of an alternating current or *a person or thing that transforms something*.

Take Scorpio Hillary Clinton. She has been the first woman in any number of areas, certainly the mark of a transformer: first student commencement speaker at Wellesley College; first female chair of the Legal Services Corporation; first female attorney at Rose Law Firm, the third oldest law firm in the U.S.; the only First Lady to be subpoenaed; first female senator from New York state; the only First Lady to ever run for public office; and in 2008, she won more primaries and delegates than any other female candidate in American history. And, if the pundits are correct, she may become the first female president in this country. Everything about her life is about transformation.

Now imagine what might happen when a pair of Scorpios taps into each other's creative energy.

Tapping In

The nature of your relationship with Scorpio will determine how this creative exchange might work. The approach of a Scorpio friend would differ from that of a parent, lover, spouse or friend.

Scorpio and Scorpio Tapping into Each Other's Creativity

A powerhouse. There's no other way to describe what happens when a pair of Scorpios tap into each other's creative energy to solve problems, brainstorm, research and find that bottom line.

Let's say you and Scorpio are friends. You're both teachers who are fascinated with ghosts, spirits and life after death. During your summer break, you decide to spend a month traveling throughout the country and visiting sites that are supposedly haunted. Scorpio suggests you two document the trip and these sites through photography, videos and a blog. You carry this idea even further by suggesting that each week you would upload the best video to YouTube and create a of serialization of your trip and search for ghosts.

> You: *Sort of like that podcast* Serial.

> Scorpio: *OMG, I love it! That's the number one download on iTunes. Everyone at work talks about it, debating whether the guy killed his girlfriend. They can't wait for the next episode. Yes, yes, let's do this!*

Fast-forward a few months. It's June, and you two are on the road. You've been uploading your videos to YouTube with riveting narratives and have even captured a number of spirits on film. The number of views on your videos is spiking each week; there's *buzz* about your serialization. By the end of the summer, your videos have received more than 20 million hits, and you're approached by a cable TV channel that offers you a price you can't refuse for continuing your videos for a new show.

What began as a fun exploration has now become a new career.

This is the sort of thing that can occur when a pair of Scorpios tap into each other's creative energy!

Sagittarius, the Traveler

Your creative theme could be encompassed in several other words—Nomad or Truth Seeker—but Traveler fits the essence. It denotes how pivotal travel is to your creativity, both physical and metaphysical travel, which is intimately connected to your search for truth. Traveler as an archetype conjures an image of a figure with a pack over his shoulder, wearing a hat and perhaps a poncho. His shoes are dusty, and the road ahead of him is long. Maybe a town or city glimmers like a mirage in the distance. The idea here is that the journey—rather than the destination—is what matters.

The image that represents your sign, the centaur with a bow and arrow, suggests a certain duality—the wild man or woman who is the complete antithesis of the conformist. The wild man is the horse part of the image, and operates from pure, raw instinct. The conformist is the human half, the part of you who is acculturated. The wild man/woman is the part of you whose creativity is born from your thirst for experience; the human part of the centaur is the part of you that takes those experiences and channels them into something tangible.

Sagittarius Shirley Jackson wasn't just the mother of four kids. She was also an accomplished writer, somewhat rare for a woman in the forties and fifties. This duality was also apparent in her professional life. She wrote lighthearted fiction for a women's magazine, but also wrote one of the darkest and most controversial short stories ever published, *The Lottery.* Her novel, *The Haunting of Hill House,* is still one of the most terrifying ghost stories ever written. As Jackson once wrote to a friend: "I delight in what I fear."

So how can Scorpio tap into your creative energy and vice versa?

Tapping In

The nature of your relationship with Scorpio will determine how this creative exchange might work. The approach of a Scorpio parent would differ from that of a friend, lover, spouse or boss.

Sagittarius and Scorpio Tapping into Each Other's Creativity

What if is your litany, your battle cry. *What if* aliens actually landed on the White House lawn? *What if* there's evidence that planes that have disappeared in the Bermuda Triangle went into a parallel dimension? *What if* the mythological gods suddenly came alive?

Let's pretend that you and Scorpio are married. She's acutely aware of all the *what-if* scenarios that drift through your head on any given day and keeps encouraging you to take at least one of those ideas and run with it.

You: *Run with it how? Where?*

Scorpio: *Write a screenplay or a novel.*

You: *I don't have the time to write.*

Scorpio: *Make the time.*

You roll your eyes and drop the subject. Several nights later over dinner you speculate about one of your favorite scenarios—*what if* dolphins worldwide joined forces and freed all the marine animals that are held in captivity for the entertainment of humans? Scorpio is prepared this time. From her handbag, she brings out two tickets to a research facility in the Florida Keys where you two are going to swim with dolphins.

The facility, she says, is not an inside aquarium where the environment is carefully regulated by computers. This place is completely outdoors; the dolphins swim in real sunlight and actual seawater that washes in through metal grates that border a canal. A week later, you swim with dolphins for the first time, and the experience is transformative, just as Scorpio knew it would be.

When you get home, you put in for your vacation leave at work and spend two weeks writing. For the next year, you write nights, weekends and whenever you have the time. You swim with dolphins several more times, read everything that author and researcher John Lilly wrote about his experiences with dolphins, travel to the Bahamas and Hawaii to experience dolphins in both of these places and then head to the Amazon to experience the pink river dolphins.

Your novel is epic, and when it's published, you're already into the second novel. You have quit your job, and you and Scorpio have moved to a cottage in the Bahamas.

And it all began that night at dinner, when Scorpio was prepared and brought out those two tickets.

Pretty cool, huh?

Capricorn, the Achiever

Few signs are capable of doing what you do, building something one careful step at a time, with a strategy or blueprint that lays out the route from A to Z. Whether you're building a career or a family, a business or an artistic project, you're methodical, persistent and consistent and rarely daunted by any obstacles you encounter. When you do encounter an obstacle, you find a way around it. Nowhere is this more apparent than in your creative expression.

Capricorn J.R.R. Tolkien, for instance, "built" the world of Middle Earth with its own language, history and mythology. He peopled it with hobbits who played out archetypal struggles between good and evil. Author Jack London, also a Capricorn, built his career with utter discipline, writing a thousand words a day, every morning without fail. In sixteen years, that came to more than fifty books, hundreds of short stories and numerous articles.

You're a cardinal earth sign ruled by Saturn, the planet that governs discipline and responsibility, qualities you have in abundance. Even when you're in the heat of creative passion, discipline is key to your success.

How can you and Scorpio tap into each other's creative energy?

Tapping In

The nature of your relationship with Scorpio will determine how this creative exchange might work. The approach of a Scorpio parent would differ from that of a friend, lover, spouse or boss.

Capricorn and Scorpio Tapping into Each Other's Creativity

Your challenge with creativity is that your sense of responsibility is so strong that you readily accept it—at home, at work, with your family and parents. Pretty soon, you're so mired in responsibility that you don't have space or time in your life for your own creativity. So let's pretend again.

Scorpio is your boss in an advertising agency. Think *Mad Men*, but set in the present. She has some great ideas about a new project the company is involved in, but you feel her ideas are impractical. Rather than *telling* her this, you *show* her by taking one of the ideas and working up an ad campaign that is both humorous and practical. You do this on your own time—at lunch, in the evenings after work, even on weekends. The end result is a mind-bending beauty that Scorpio loves—and you get a promotion.

Now let's turn the tables. You're the boss, and Scorpio is the employee. You've been working fifty-hour weeks, have a family and aging parents who require your attention and are rapidly approaching burnout. Scorpio picks up on this and steps in with a suggestion that the company hire a meditation teacher who would come in several times a week and hold a meditation class for anyone who wants to attend. At first, you balk. *We can't afford it. We can't do this during office hours. No, no, no.* Scorpio brings out article after article that cite the health and creative benefits of meditation. You finally relent. *We'll try it for one week.*

After that first week, you're not only convinced of the merits of meditation, your brain is practically bursting with ideas. Your employees are more productive, and you're able to cope better with all your responsibilities. Your health improves, and there are numerous other tangible, practical benefits.

Aquarius, the Visionary

Thanks to your curiosity about life and its mysteries, you may excel creatively in more than just one area. In fact, maintaining this curiosity is vital to your creativity. It kicks you out of the rut of rigid opinions and beliefs into which many fixed signs fall. *What does that mean? Why is this happening?* You then set out to answer these questions.

As a sign ruled by Uranus, your creativity often has an eccentric edge to it and may, in some way, break with the traditions in which you were raised. Take Aquarius Charles Darwin. When he was sixteen, he went off to medical school to become a doctor like his father, but was so repelled by the sight of surgery performed without anesthesia that he left medical school to become a clergyman. At the age of twenty-two, he had a chance to work as an unpaid naturalist on the HMS *Beagle* for a five-year scientific expedition to the Pacific coast of South America. The research from this voyage provided the basis for his groundbreaking and controversial book, *On the Origin of Species*, which ultimately transformed the scientific thought of the era.

Whether your creative theme is called visionary or paradigm-busting, they amount to the same thing. By following your vision of what might be, you often shatter old notions and beliefs and usher in new ways of being.

How can you and Scorpio tap into each other's creative energy?

Tapping In
The nature of your relationship with Scorpio will determine how this creative exchange might work. The approach of a Scorpio spouse would differ from that of a friend, lover, colleague or boss.

Aquarius and Scorpio Tapping into Each Other's Creativity
Your ruler, Uranus, is a highly charged planet that governs lightning, explosive events, the abrupt and unexpected, new technologies and scientific genius. It kicks us out of our ruts, routines and established ways of being and *wakes us up* so that we can embrace and achieve all of our potential.

And you ask, *What potential is that?*

Let's play the pretend game again. You and Scorpio are colleagues at the same high school. You teach English and Scorpio teaches history. Neither of you is satisfied with your job—the bureaucracy, teaching to standardized tests and the often ridiculous requirements. It all stifles creativity—in both of you and in your students. One day after school, you and Scorpio brainstorm about how to improve your jobs/careers.

You: *Last night I bolted awake with an idea. Want to hear it?*

Scorpio: *Of course.*

You: *You and I should propose a school trip that combines English and history.*

Scorpio: *A trip to where?*

You: *England, to visit places like Stonehenge. Twenty students max. They have to write a thesis on the trip that combines English and history.*

Scorpio: *How long a trip?*

You: *Ten days.*

Scorpio: *Let's make it a semester abroad.*

You: *Fantastic!*

You discuss the details, who will do what, where everyone will live during this semester abroad and what the expense might be. You both write up a proposal to present to the principal and talk about it in your classes. To your surprise, the principal loves the idea. Gradually, all the pieces come together, and students are clamoring for this semester abroad.

And it started because you awakened one night with an idea!

Pisces, the Healer/Psychic

Like your mutable cousin, Gemini, your sign is also depicted by a double image—of a pair of fish swimming in opposite directions—so you also get two creative themes. The healer theme runs throughout everything you do. You hear a sob story from a friend, and your compassion immediately reaches out to comfort and heal the person's sadness. You find a stray kitten and take it home. You see a young family begging at the side of the road and stop to give them money.

In a larger sense, you seek to heal humanity's wounds. Michelangelo did it by creating breathtaking art that transports us. Beatle George Harrison did it through the exquisite music he created. For Einstein, the healing lay in his relativity theory, which changed the way we saw the world.

The Psychic archetype, your second theme, is the wellspring of your creativity. Your intuitive ability enables you to reach out through time and space for ideas and insights to connect with your higher self, soul or the divine. Pisces Edgar Cayce, known as the Sleeping Prophet, was the most famous and documented psychic of the twentieth century. He would put himself in a light sleep state that enabled him to "read" an individual based on nothing more than the person's name and location. He did more than 14,000 of these readings, and true to the dual creative themes of his sign, many of them were about health and healing.

How can you and Scorpio tap into each other's creativity? Since you're both water signs, it should be fairly simple.

Tapping In

The nature of your relationship with Scorpio will determine how this creative exchange might work. The approach of a Scorpio friend would differ from that of a spouse, lover, colleague or boss.

Pisces and Scorpio Tapping into Each Other's Creativity

Your ruler, Neptune, has something of a dual nature, just as you do. Neptune governs illusions, delusion, escapism and addiction. But it also governs our higher selves, artistic inspiration, dreams, films, mysticism and the paranormal. The influence of Neptune is why some people describe you as dreamy, spacey, mysterious and enigmatic.

Let's say that you and Scorpio are friends. She's in love with a guy who may or may not feel the same way about her and is driving herself nuts trying to figure out where the relationship is headed. So she asks you what you think.

Scorpio: *You get feelings about things. What do you feel about this relationship I'm in?*

You: *Hey, you're more intuitive than I am. What do you feel about it?*

Scorpio: *My feelings are too mixed up. I can't get any clarity on this. Read the cards for me.*

You bring out your deck of tarot cards, tell Scorpio to think about her question and draw six cards. She fans out the deck and moves her hands over the cards, waiting for that nudge that whispers, *Me, choose me.*

The cards she has drawn tell a story, and it sure doesn't look good. You would like to sugar coat this for her so she isn't hurt, but that would be dishonest. She senses your hesitation and says, "Just tell me the truth."

"He's seeing someone else."

Scorpio just sits there, staring at the cards and then raises her eyes. "I knew it," she says softly. "You've just saved me a world of more heartache."

The next morning, Scorpio calls to tell you she confronted the guy, and he admitted that he was seeing someone else.

Acknowledgments

Thank you to my agent, Al Zuckerman—a Virgo extraordinaire—and to Scorpio Will Kiester, who came up with the idea. I'd also like to thank the moms of Scorpio children who shared their experiences: my sister Mary Anderson, Carol Bowman and Julie Scully.

About the Author

Trish MacGregor was born and raised in Caracas, Venezuela. She now lives in South Florida with her husband, novelist Rob MacGregor, daughter Megan, two cats and a noble Golden Retriever.

For a decade, she and her husband wrote the Sydney Omarr series of astrology books. She has also written a dozen other books on various facets of astrology, on the tarot, dreams and synchronicity. As T.J. MacGregor, she's the author of 39 novels that have been translated into fifteen languages.

If you'd like to get more information about astrology, or if you'd like to contact Trish, please visit her website www.synchrosecrets.com.

Index